MASTER THE™ DSST®

Astronomy Exam

About Peterson's

Peterson's® has been your trusted educational publisher for over 50 years. It's a milestone we're quite proud of, as we continue to offer the most accurate, dependable, high-quality educational content in the field, providing you with everything you need to succeed. No matter where you are on your academic or professional path, you can rely on Peterson's for its books, online information, expert test-prep tools, the most up-to-date education exploration data, and the highest quality career success resources—everything you need to achieve your education goals. For our complete line of products, visit www.petersons.com.

For more information, contact Peterson's, 8740 Lucent Blvd., Suite 400, Highlands Ranch, CO 80129; 800-338-3282 Ext. 54229; or find us online at **www.petersons.com**.

ISBN: 978-0-7689-4446-4

Printed in the United States of America

10 9 8 7 6 5 4 3 2 1 22 21 20

Contents

Before You Begin

HOW THIS BOOK IS ORGANIZED

Peterson's *Master the™ DSST® Astronomy Exam* provides a diagnostic test, subject-matter review, and a post-test.

- **Diagnostic Test**—Twenty multiple-choice questions, followed by an answer key with detailed answer explanations
- **Assessment Grid**—A chart designed to help you identify areas that you need to focus on based on your test results
- **Subject-Matter Review**—General overview of the exam subject, followed by a review of the relevant topics and terminology covered on the exam
- **Post-Test**—Sixty multiple-choice questions, followed by an answer key and detailed answer explanations

The purpose of the diagnostic test is to help you figure out what you know—or don't know. The twenty multiple-choice questions are similar to the ones found on the DSST exam, and they should provide you with a good idea of what to expect. Once you take the diagnostic test, check your answers to see how you did. Included with each correct answer is a brief explanation regarding why a specific answer is correct, and in many cases, why other options are incorrect. Use the assessment grid to identify the questions you miss so that you can spend more time reviewing that information later. As with any exam, knowing your weak spots greatly improves your chances of success.

Following the diagnostic test is a subject-matter review. The review summarizes the various topics covered on the DSST exam. Key terms are defined, important concepts are explained, and, when appropriate, examples are provided. As you read the review, some of the information may seem familiar while other information may seem foreign. Again, take note of the unfamiliar because that will most likely cause you problems on the actual exam.

After studying the subject-matter review, you should be ready for the post-test. The post-test contains sixty multiple-choice items, and it will serve as a dry run for the real DSST exam. There are complete answer explanations at the end of the test.

OTHER DSST PRODUCTS BY PETERSON'S

Books, flashcards, practice tests, and videos available online at **www.petersons.com/testprep/dsst**

- Art of the Western World
- Astronomy
- Business Mathematics
- Business Ethics and Society
- Civil War and Reconstruction
- Computing and Information Technology
- Criminal Justice
- Environmental Science
- Ethics in America
- Ethics in Technology
- Foundations of Education
- Fundamentals of College Algebra
- Fundamentals of Counseling
- Fundamentals of Cybersecurity
- General Anthropology
- Health and Human Development
- History of the Soviet Union
- History of the Vietnam War
- Human Resource Management
- Introduction to Business
- Introduction to Geography
- Introduction to Geology
- Introduction to Law Enforcement
- Introduction to World Religions
- Lifespan Developmental Psychology
- Math for Liberal Arts
- Management Information Systems
- Money and Banking
- Organizational Behavior
- Personal Finance
- Principles of Advanced English Composition
- Principles of Finance
- Principles of Public Speaking
- Principles of Statistics
- Principles of Supervision
- Substance Abuse
- Technical Writing

Chapter 1

All About the DSST® Exam

WHAT IS DSST®?

Previously known as the DANTES Subject Standardized Tests, the DSST program provides the opportunity for individuals to earn college credit for what they have learned outside the traditional classroom. Accepted or administered at over 1,900 colleges and universities nationwide and approved by the American Council on Education (ACE), the DSST program enables individuals to use the knowledge they have acquired outside the classroom to accomplish their educational and professional goals.

WHY TAKE A DSST® EXAM?

DSST exams offer a way for you to save both time and money in your quest for a college education. Why enroll in a college course in a subject you already understand? For over 30 years, the DSST program has offered the perfect solution for individuals who are knowledgeable in a specific subject and want to save both time and money. A passing score on a DSST exam provides physical evidence to universities of proficiency in a specific subject. Over 1,900 accredited and respected colleges and universities across the nation award undergraduate credit for passing scores on DSST exams. With the DSST program, individuals can shave months off the time it takes to earn a degree.

The DSST program offers numerous advantages for individuals in all stages of their educational development:

- Adult learners
- College students
- Military personnel

Adult learners desiring college degrees face unique circumstances like demanding work schedules, family responsibilities, and tight budgets. Yet adult learners also have years of valuable work experience that can be applied toward a degree through the DSST program. For example, adult learners with on-the-job experience in business and management might be able to skip the Business 101 courses if they earn passing marks on DSST exams such as Introduction to Business and Principles of Supervision.

Adult learners can put their prior learning into action and move forward with more advanced coursework. Adults who have never enrolled in a college course may feel a little uncertain about their abilities. If this describes your situation, then sign up for a DSST exam and see how you do. A passing score may be the boost you need to realize your dream of earning a degree. With family and work commitments, adult learners often feel they lack the time to attend college. The DSST program enables adult learners the unique opportunity to work toward college degrees without the time constraints of semester-long coursework. DSST exams take two hours or less to complete. In one weekend, you could earn credit for multiple college courses.

The DSST exams also benefit students who are already enrolled in a college or university. With college tuition costs on the rise, most students face financial challenges. The fee for each DSST exam starts at $80 (plus administration fees charged by some testing facilities)—significantly less than the $750 average cost of a 3-hour college class. Maximize tuition assistance by taking DSST exams for introductory or mandatory course work. Once you earn a passing score on a DSST exam, then you are free to move on to higher-level course work in that subject matter, take desired electives, or focus on courses in a chosen major.

Not only do college students and adult learners profit from DSST exams, but military personnel reap the benefits as well. If you are a member of the armed services at home or abroad, you can initiate your post-military career by taking DSST exams in areas with which you have experience. Military personnel can gain credit anywhere in the world, thanks to the fact that almost all of the tests are available through the internet at designated testing locations. DSST testing facilities are located at over 500 military installations, so service members on active duty can get a jump-start on a post-military career with the DSST program. As an additional incentive, DANTES (Defense Activity for Non-Traditional Education Support) provides funding for DSST test fees for eligible members of the military.

More than 30 subject-matter tests are available in the fields of Business, Humanities, Math, Physical Science, Social Sciences, and Technology.

Available DSST® Exams

Business	Social Sciences
Business Ethics and Society Business Mathematics Computing and Information Technology Human Resource Management Introduction to Business Management Information Systems Money and Banking Organizational Behavior Personal Finance Principles of Finance Principles of Supervision	A History of the Vietnam War Art of the Western World Criminal Justice Foundations of Education Fundamentals of Counseling General Anthropology History of the Soviet Union Introduction to Geography Introduction to Law Enforcement Lifespan Developmental Psychology Substance Abuse The Civil War and Reconstruction
Humanities	**Physical Sciences**
Ethics in America Introduction to World Religions Principles of Advanced English Composition Principles of Public Speaking	Astronomy Environmental Science Health and Human Development Introduction to Geology
Math	**Technology**
Fundamentals of College Algebra Math for Liberal Arts Principles of Statistics	Ethics in Technology Fundamentals of Cybersecurity Technical Writing

As you can see from the table, the DSST program covers a wide variety of subjects. However, it is important to ask two questions before registering for a DSST exam.

1. Which universities or colleges award credit for passing DSST exams?
2. Which DSST exams are the most relevant to my desired degree and my experience?

Knowing which universities offer DSST credit is important. In all likelihood, a college in your area awards credit for DSST exams, but find out before taking an exam by contacting the university directly. Then review the list of DSST exams to determine which ones are most relevant to the degree you are seeking and to your base of knowledge. Schedule an appointment with your college adviser to determine which exams best fit your degree program, and which college courses the DSST exams can replace. Advisers should also be able to tell you the minimum score required on the DSST exam to receive university credit.

DSST® TEST CENTERS

You can find DSST testing locations in community colleges and universities across the country. Contact your local college or university to find out if the school administers DSST exams or check the DSST website (**www.getcollegecredit.com**) for a location near you. Keep in mind that some universities and colleges administer DSST exams only to enrolled students. DSST testing is available to men and women in the armed services at over 500 military installations around the world.

HOW TO REGISTER FOR A DSST® EXAM

Once you have located a nearby DSST testing facility, you need to contact the testing center to find out the exam administration schedule. Many centers are set up to administer tests via the internet, while others use printed materials. Almost all DSST exams are available as online tests, but the method used depends on the testing center. The cost for each DSST exam starts at $80, and many testing locations charge a fee to cover their costs for administering the tests. Credit cards are the only accepted payment method for taking online DSST exams. Credit card, certified check, and money order are acceptable payment methods for paper-and-pencil tests.

Test takers are allotted two score reports—one mailed to them and another mailed to a designated college or university by request. Online tests generate unofficial scores at the end of the test session, while individuals taking paper tests must wait four to six weeks for score reports.

PREPARING FOR A DSST® EXAM

Even though you are knowledgeable in a certain subject matter, you should still prepare for the test to ensure you achieve the highest score possible. The first step in studying for a DSST exam is to find out what will be on the specific test you have chosen. Information regarding test content is located on the DSST fact sheets, which can be downloaded at no cost from **www.getcollegecredit.com**. Each fact sheet outlines the topics covered on a subject-matter test, as well as the approximate percentage assigned to each topic. For example, questions on the Substance Abuse exam are distributed in the following way: 12% on overview of substance abuse and dependence; 6% on classification of drugs; 6% on pharmacological and neurophysiological principles; 14% on alcohol; 6% on anti-anxiety sedatives and hypnotics; 6% on inhalants; 10% on tobacco and nicotine; 6% on psychomotor stimulants; 8% on opioids; 11% on cannabinoids; 4% on hallucinogens; 4% on other drugs of abuse; 3% on antipsychotic drugs; and 4% on antidepressants and mood stabilizers.

In addition to the breakdown of topics on a DSST exam, the fact sheet also lists recommended reference materials. If you do not own the recommended books, then check college bookstores. Avoid paying high prices for new textbooks by looking online for used textbooks. Don't panic if you are unable to locate a specific textbook listed on the fact sheet; the textbooks are merely recommendations. Instead, search for comparable books used in university courses on the specific subject. Current editions are ideal, and it is a good idea to use at least two references when studying for a DSST exam. Of course, the subject matter provided in this book will be a sufficient review for most test takers. However, if you need additional information, then it is a good idea to have some of the reference materials at your disposal when preparing for a DSST exam.

Fact sheets include other useful information in addition to a list of reference materials and topics. Each fact sheet includes subject-specific sample questions like those you will encounter on the DSST exam. The sample questions provide an idea of the types of questions you can expect on the exam. Test questions are multiple-choice with one correct answer and three incorrect choices.

The fact sheet also includes information about the number of credit hours that ACE has recommended be awarded by colleges for a passing DSST exam score. However, you should keep in mind that not all universities and colleges adhere to the the American Council on Education (ACE) recommendation for DSST credit hours. Some institutions require DSST exam scores higher than the minimum score recommended by ACE. Once you have acquired appropriate reference materials and you have the outline provided on the fact sheet, you are ready to start studying, which is where this book can help.

TEST DAY

After reviewing the material and taking practice tests, you are finally ready to take your DSST exam. Follow these tips for a successful test day experience.

1. **Arrive on time.** Not only is it courteous to arrive on time to the DSST testing facility, but it also allows plenty of time for you to take care of check-in procedures and settle into your surroundings.
2. **Bring identification.** DSST test facilities require that candidates bring a valid government-issued identification card with a current photo and signature. Acceptable forms of identification include a current driver's license, passport, military identification card, or state-issued identification card. Individuals who fail to bring proper identification to the DSST testing facility will not be allowed to take an exam.
3. **Bring the right supplies.** If your exam requires the use of a calculator, you may bring a calculator that meets the specifications. For paper-based exams, you may also bring No. 2 pencils with an eraser and black ballpoint pens. Regardless of the exam methodology, you are NOT allowed to bring reference or study materials, scratch paper, or electronics such as cell phones, personal handheld devices, cameras, alarm wrist watches, or tape recorders to the testing center.
4. **Take the test.** During the exam, take the time to read each question-and-answer option carefully. Eliminate the choices you know are incorrect to narrow the number of potential answers. If a question completely stumps you, take an educated guess and move on—remember that DSSTs are timed; you will have 2 hours to take the exam.

With the proper preparation, DSST exams will save you both time and money. So join the thousands of people who have already reaped the benefits of DSST exams and move closer than ever to your college degree.

ASTRONOMY EXAM FACTS

This exam was developed to enable schools to award credit to students for knowledge equivalent to that learned by students taking the course. The DSST Astronomy exam consists of 100 multiple-choice questions and includes topics such as astrophysics; celestial systems; the science of light; planetary systems; and the nature and evolution of the sun and stars, galaxies, and the universe.

Area or Course Equivalent: Astronomy
Level: Lower-level baccalaureate
Amount of Credit: 3 Semester Hours
Minimum Score: 400
Source: https://www.getcollegecredit.com/wp-content/assets/factsheets/Astronomy.pdf

I. Introduction to the Science of Astronomy – 5%
   a. Nature and methods of science
   b. Applications of scientific thinking
   c. History of early astronomy

II. Astrophysics – 15%
   a. Kepler's laws and orbits
   b. Newtonian physics and gravity
   c. Relativity

III. Celestial Systems – 10%
   a. Celestial motions
   b. Earth and the moon
   c. Seasons, calendar, and time keeping

IV. The Science of Light – 15%
   a. The electromagnetic spectrum
   b. Telescopes and the measurement of light
   c. Spectroscopy
   d. Blackbody radiation

V. Planetary Systems: Our Solar System and Others – 20%
   a. Contents of our solar system
   b. Formation and evolution of planetary systems
   c. Exoplanets
   d. Habitability and life in the universe

VI. The Sun and Stars: Nature and Evolution – 15%
   a. Our Star, the sun
   b. Properties and classification of stars
   c. Birth, life, and death of stars
   d. Nuclear fusion and the origin of elements

VII. Galaxies – 10%

   a. Our Galaxy: The Milky Way
   b. Classification and structure of galaxies
   c. Measuring cosmic distances

VIII. The Universe: Contents, Structure, and Evolution – 10%

   a. Galaxy clusters and large-scale structure
   b. The Big Bang and Hubble's law
   c. The evolution and fate of the universe
   d. Dark matter and dark energy

Chapter 2

Astronomy Diagnostic Test

DIAGNOSTIC TEST ANSWER SHEET

1. Ⓐ Ⓑ Ⓒ Ⓓ
2. Ⓐ Ⓑ Ⓒ Ⓓ
3. Ⓐ Ⓑ Ⓒ Ⓓ
4. Ⓐ Ⓑ Ⓒ Ⓓ
5. Ⓐ Ⓑ Ⓒ Ⓓ
6. Ⓐ Ⓑ Ⓒ Ⓓ
7. Ⓐ Ⓑ Ⓒ Ⓓ
8. Ⓐ Ⓑ Ⓒ Ⓓ
9. Ⓐ Ⓑ Ⓒ Ⓓ
10. Ⓐ Ⓑ Ⓒ Ⓓ
11. Ⓐ Ⓑ Ⓒ Ⓓ
12. Ⓐ Ⓑ Ⓒ Ⓓ
13. Ⓐ Ⓑ Ⓒ Ⓓ
14. Ⓐ Ⓑ Ⓒ Ⓓ
15. Ⓐ Ⓑ Ⓒ Ⓓ
16. Ⓐ Ⓑ Ⓒ Ⓓ
17. Ⓐ Ⓑ Ⓒ Ⓓ
18. Ⓐ Ⓑ Ⓒ Ⓓ
19. Ⓐ Ⓑ Ⓒ Ⓓ
20. Ⓐ Ⓑ Ⓒ Ⓓ

ASTRONOMY DIAGNOSTIC TEST

Directions: Carefully read each of the following 20 questions. Choose the best answer to each question and fill in the corresponding circle on the answer sheet. The Answer Key and Explanations can be found following this Diagnostic Test.

1. When is the sun directly above your head if you are in the continental United States?

A. Every day at noon
B. Only on the first day of summer
C. Only on the first day of winter
D. Never in the continental United States

2. When we have a lunar eclipse, what is the phase of the moon?

A. Full
B. New
C. First quarter
D. Third quarter

3. You have two balls of equal size, but ball A is twice as massive as ball B. If you take the balls and you let them fall, what will happen after five seconds (ignoring air resistance)?

A. Ball A will reach the ground twice as fast as ball B.
B. Ball A will reach the ground four times faster than ball B.
C. Ball B will reach the ground twice as fast as ball A.
D. They will reach the ground at the same time.

4. How does the speed of radio waves compare to the speed of visible light?

A. Radio waves are much slower than visible light.
B. They both travel at the same speed.
C. Radio waves are much faster than visible light.
D. Radio waves are only slightly slower than visible light.

5. Astronauts inside the space shuttle float because

A. there is no gravity in space.
B. they are falling in the same way as the space shuttle.
C. they are above the earth's atmosphere.
D. there is less gravity inside the space shuttle than outside.

6. Imagine that the earth's orbit was changed to be a perfect circle around the sun so that the distance to the sun never changed. How would this affect the seasons?

A. We would no longer experience a difference between the seasons.
B. We would still experience seasons, but the difference would be much LESS noticeable.
C. We would still experience seasons, but the difference would be much MORE noticeable.
D. We would continue to experience seasons in the same way we do now.

7. Where does the sun's energy come from?

A. The combining of light elements into heavier elements
B. The breaking apart of heavy elements into lighter ones
C. Radioactive decay of heavy elements
D. Heat left over from the formation of the sun

8. On the fall equinox, the sun sets directly west. Where would the sun appear to set two weeks later?

A. Directly west
B. In the southwest
C. In the northwest
D. In the east

9. Compared to the distance to the moon, how far away is the space shuttle (when in space) from the earth?

A. Very close to the earth
B. About halfway to the moon
C. Very close to the moon
D. About twice as far as the moon

10. As viewed from our location, the stars of the Big Dipper can be connected with imaginary lines to form the shape of a pot with a curved handle. Where would you have to travel to first observe a considerable change in the shape formed by these stars?

A. Across the country
B. A distant star
C. The moon
D. Pluto

11. A person is reading a newspaper while standing five feet away from a table that has on it an unshaded 100-watt light bulb. Imagine that the table was moved to a distance of ten feet. How many light bulbs in total would have to be placed on the table to light up the newspaper to the same amount of brightness as before?

A. One bulb
B. Two bulbs
C. Three bulbs
D. Four bulbs

12. According to modern ideas and observations, what is present at the center of the universe?

A. The sun is at the center.
B. The Milky Way galaxy is at the center.
C. An unknown, distant galaxy is at the center.
D. The universe does not have a center.

13. The coldest stars are what color?

A. Blue
B. Orange
C. Red
D. Yellow

14. Which of the following stars will end their lives as black holes?

A. B stars
B. F stars
C. G stars
D. M stars

15. Global warming is thought to be caused by the

A. destruction of the ozone layer.
B. trapping of heat by nitrogen.
C. addition of carbon dioxide in the atmosphere.
D. increased oxygen in the atmosphere.

16. The first person to present the law of inertia was

A. Isaac Newton
B. Tycho Brahe
C. Galileo Galilei
D. Rene Descartes

17. What are the two main types of planets in the solar system?

A. Terrestrial and Jovian planets
B. Terrestrial and dwarf planets
C. Rocky and metallic planets
D. Habitable and terrestrial planets

18. Where are comets found most of the time?

A. Near the sun
B. Between Mercury and Mars
C. Between Jupiter and Neptune
D. Beyond Neptune

19. What is parallax?

A. The apparent retrograde motion of planets because we are moving
B. The apparent shift in the position of stars because we are moving
C. A method to estimate the proper motion of stars
D. A method to calculate distances to galaxies

20. What is our cosmic address?

A. Earth, solar system, Milky Way galaxy, Local Group, Virgo Supercluster, universe
B. Earth, Milky Way galaxy, solar system, Local Group, Virgo Supercluster, universe
C. Earth, solar system, Local Group, Virgo Supercluster, Milky Way galaxy, universe
D. Earth, Local Group, Virgo Supercluster, solar system, Milky Way galaxy, universe

ANSWER KEY AND EXPLANATIONS

1. D	5. B	9. A	13. C	17. A
2. A	6. D	10. B	14. A	18. D
3. D	7. A	11. D	15. C	19. B
4. B	8. B	12. D	16. C	20. A

1. **The correct answer is D.** The sun will be highest in the sky on the summer solstice, when it is directly overhead at the Tropic of Cancer, latitude 23.5 degrees north. Since the continental United States is at higher latitudes than the Tropic of Cancer, the sun is never directly overhead. Even though the sun is highest in the sky at local noon (choice A), it is never high enough in the United States to be overhead. On the first day of summer (choice B), the summer solstice, the sun is highest in the sky in the Northern Hemisphere, but it is still not directly overhead unless you are in the Tropic of Cancer. On the first day of winter (choice C), the winter solstice, the sun is lowest in the sky, but still is directly overhead only in the Tropic of Capricorn, latitude 23.5 degrees south.

2. **The correct answer is A.** During a lunar eclipse, the earth gets in between the moon and the sun, and its shadow falls on the moon, creating a lunar eclipse. Since the moon and the sun are 180 degrees away from each other with the earth in between, the phase of the moon is full. When the moon is new (choice B), the moon is in between the earth and the sun, and a lunar eclipse cannot take place. When the moon is either first quarter (choice C) or third quarter (choice D), the angle between the sun, earth, and moon is either 90 degrees or 270 degrees, so they are not aligned, and the shadow of the earth cannot fall on the moon to create an eclipse.

3. **The correct answer is D.** The two balls will fall at the same rate and reach the ground at the same time (if we ignore air resistance). This is the law of free fall discovered by Galileo Galilei. Choices A and B are incorrect because the heavier ball doesn't fall faster, and choice C is incorrect because the lighter ball doesn't fall faster.

4. **The correct answer is B.** Radio waves and visible light are part of the electromagnetic spectrum, and they both travel at the speed of light. Choices A, C, and D are incorrect because all parts of spectrum travel at the same speed.

5. **The correct answer is B.** The space shuttle, and everything in it, is constantly falling toward earth, which is why astronauts experience weightlessness inside the space station. Gravity doesn't disappear in space (choice A). The force of gravity becomes weaker with distance, but it is still there making the space shuttle orbit the earth. The earth's atmosphere (choice C) doesn't affect gravity. Gravity is the same inside and outside the space shuttle (choice D), since they are at the same distance from earth.

6. **The correct answer is D.** The eccentricity of the earth's orbit is very small, so the earth's orbit is already very close to a circle. We have seasons because the earth's axis is inclined 23.5 degrees relative to the ecliptic and not because of the changing distance from the earth to the sun. Therefore, if the earth's orbit were a perfect circle, the effect on the seasons would be very small, and we would continue to experience seasons in the same way we do right now. Choice A is incorrect because seasons are the result of the axis tilt of earth and not the eccentricity of the earth's orbit. Choices B and C are incorrect because the effect of having a circular orbit on the seasons would be negligible.

7. **The correct answer is A.** The sun's energy comes from fusing lighter elements into heavier elements. Neither the breaking of heavy elements into lighter ones (choice B) nor radioactive decay (choice C) are responsible for the energy produced in the sun. The heat left over from the formation of sun (choice D) is not enough to power the sun.

8. **The correct answer is B.** The sun sets directly west on the fall equinox, after which the setting point of the sun moves southwest until winter solstice, when it reaches its maximum distance away from west. The sun sets directly west (choice A) only on the fall and spring equinoxes, and it sets in the northwest (choice C) after the spring equinox (between March 22 and September 20). The sun never sets in the east (choice D).

9. **The correct answer is A.** The space station is only about 400 km away, which is very close to earth. The space shuttle is always somewhere between those two points, so it never goes far from earth. The moon is about 384,000 km away from the earth, or 30 times the earth's diameter. All artificial satellites are very close to earth if we compare them with the distance to the moon, and therefore all the other answers are incorrect.

10. **The correct answer is B.** The stars in the Big Dipper are extremely far away; therefore, to see a large change in the shape of constellations, one would have to view them from far away in the solar system, on another star. Choices A, C, and D are incorrect because the distances between Earth, the moon, and Pluto are negligible compared to the distances to stars, and we would not see a big change in the shape made by the stars from those locations.

11. **The correct answer is D.** If the distance is double, the brightness we receive will decrease by four (the square of two); therefore, we would need four bulbs to receive the same amount of light. All the other choices are incorrect.

12. **The correct answer is D.** The universe doesn't have a center, and it is expanding in all directions in the same way. Choices A, B, and C are incorrect because there is no center of the universe.

13. **The correct answer is C.** The coolest color that we can see in visible light is red; therefore, the coldest stars will be seen as red stars. Choice A is incorrect because blue stars will be the hottest stars. Choices B and D are incorrect because these stars will have intermediate temperatures.

14. **The correct answer is A.** Only the most massive stars—stars of spectral types O and B— will end their lives as black holes. Choices B, C, and D are not correct because stars of spectral types F, G, and M are not massive enough to end their lives as black holes.

15. **The correct answer is C.** Accumulation of greenhouse gasses like carbon dioxide in the atmosphere reinforces the greenhouse effect, making the temperature of the planet rise. Neither ozone (choice A), nitrogen (choice B), nor oxygen (choice D) are major greenhouse gasses.

16. **The correct answer is C.** Galileo Galilei developed the first law of inertia after experimenting with inclined planes. His law of inertia applied to motion on the horizontal plane. Newton (choice A) only expanded on the law of inertia already proposed by Galileo and Descartes. Tycho Brahe (choice B) never proposed a law of inertia. Descartes (choice D) generalized Galileo's law of inertia so that it applied not only to motion on the horizontal plane, but to objects moving in any direction or at rest.

17. **The correct answer is A.** Planets in our solar system are classified into two categories. Terrestrial planets are made mostly of rocks and metals, and Jovian planets are mostly hydrogen and helium. Dwarf planets (choice B) like Ceres and Pluto are objects that have not cleared their orbit of other objects, and are therefore not considered main planets. Rocky and metallic (choice C) are not categories of planets. Habitable (choice D) means that a planet is in the habitable area around a star; it is not a type of planet. A planet can be terrestrial or Jovian and be in the habitable zone.

18. **The correct answer is D.** Comets are found in the Kuiper Belt beyond the orbit of Neptune and in the Oort cloud, even farther away. Choices A and B are incorrect because only some comets have orbits that bring them into the inner solar system for a short amount of time. Choice C is incorrect because both the Kuiper Belt and the Oort cloud are beyond Neptune's orbit and not in between Jupiter and Neptune.

19. **The correct answer is B.** Parallax is the apparent shift of the position of a star relative to stars in the background because our line of sight changes as the earth orbits the sun. Retrograde motion (choice A) is related to the motion of the earth and other planets around the sun; it is not related to parallax. Parallax doesn't give us the real motion of stars (choice C) relative to the sun; parallax is only due to the earth orbiting the sun. Galaxies (choice D) are so far away that we cannot measure the parallax angle to stars in other galaxies.

20. **The correct answer is A.** Our cosmic address begins with our planet and gives our position in order of increasing size. Therefore, the correct order will be planet Earth, which is part of the solar system, which is part of the Milky Way galaxy, which is located in the Local Group of galaxies, which is part of the Virgo Supercluster, which is part of the universe. Choices B, C, and D give the address in the wrong order.

DIAGNOSTIC TEST ASSESSMENT GRID

Now that you've completed the diagnostic test and read through the answer explanations, you can use your results to target your studying. Find the question numbers from the diagnostic test that you answered incorrectly and highlight or circle them below. Then focus extra attention on the sections dealing with those topics.

Astronomy		
Content Area	**Topic**	**Question #**
Introduction to the Science of Astronomy	• Nature and methods of science • Applications of scientific thinking • History of early astronomy	16
Astrophysics	• Kepler's laws and orbits • Newtonian physics and gravity • Relativity	3, 5
Celestial Systems	• Celestial motions • Earth and the moon • Seasons, calendar, and time keeping	1, 2, 6, 8, 9, 15
The Science of Light	• The electromagnetic spectrum • Telescopes and the measurement of light • Spectroscopy • Blackbody radiation	4, 11, 13
Planetary Systems: Our Solar System and Others	• Contents of our solar system • Formation and evolution of planetary systems • Exoplanets • Habitability and life in the universe	17, 18
The Sun and Stars: Nature and Evolution	• Our star, the sun • Properties and classification of stars • Birth, life, and death of stars • Nuclear fusion and the origin of the elements	7, 10, 14

Galaxies	• Our Galaxy: the Milky Way • Classification and structure of galaxies • Measuring cosmic distances	19
The Universe: Content, Structure, and Evolution	• Galaxy clusters and large-scale structure • The big bang and Hubble's law • The evolution and fate of the universe • Dark matter and dark energy	12, 20

Chapter 3

Astronomy Subject Review

INTRODUCTION TO THE SCIENCE OF ASTRONOMY

Nature and Methods of Science

The Scientific Method

The **scientific method** is an approach to investigation of the world around us involving both thinking and doing. Phenomena are carefully observed, explained via theories, and those theories are tested via experiment, producing more observations, which in turn can be used to predict more phenomena. It's important to note that this cycle can begin at any of these points: observation, theory, or prediction. It is also important to realize that the cycle is never-ending, continuing as theories are refined and tested, and new phenomena are discovered that require explanation.

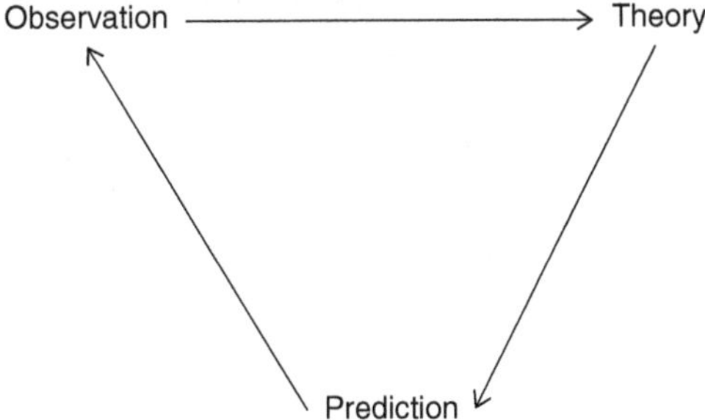

Applications of Scientific Thinking

Occam's Razor

The fourteenth-century English Franciscan friar and philosopher William of Ockham formulated a problem-solving principle known as **Occam's**

razor. The principle states that "entities should not be multiplied unnecessarily," or, put more simply and applied to science, *if there are multiple ways to explain a phenomenon, the simplest explanation tends to be correct.*

Scientific Theories

A **scientific theory** is a way to take ideas and observations of a real-world phenomenon and use them to make predictions. Application of the theory results in a **theoretical model** of the phenomenon that explains existing data, predicts future results, and can direct new avenues of inquiry. A scientific theory has several defining characteristics:

1. **A theory must be *testable*.** Any proper theory must be able to be subjected to experimental verification or rejection in order for the scientific method to work. Ideas may be untestable because they are beyond our current ability to test, are inherently untestable, or are pseudoscientific. In all of those cases, the idea in question cannot form the basis of scientific inquiry.
2. **A theory must be *tested*.** Scientific theories must be tested via the scientific method to be of any use. Theories are continually compared to observational data to determine their validity. Any single wrong prediction or inexplicable datum can serve to invalidate a theory. Thus, we can never say that a theory is *true*, just that it is widely accepted and repeatedly confirmed. This lack of absolute truth doesn't stop theories from being used to make the most accurate predictions and serve as the basis of all of modern technology.
3. **A theory must be *simple*.** According to Occam's razor, the simplest scientific theory to explain all the available observational data is likely the correct one. At the least, additional complexity requires additional predictive power. Adding more variables than necessary to fit data leads to *overfitting*, which in turn leads to poor predictive power in a model. Looking at the graph of overfitted data versus linear data, we see that although the complex polynomial model fits all the data exactly, the linear model is likely to be a better prediction of future data.

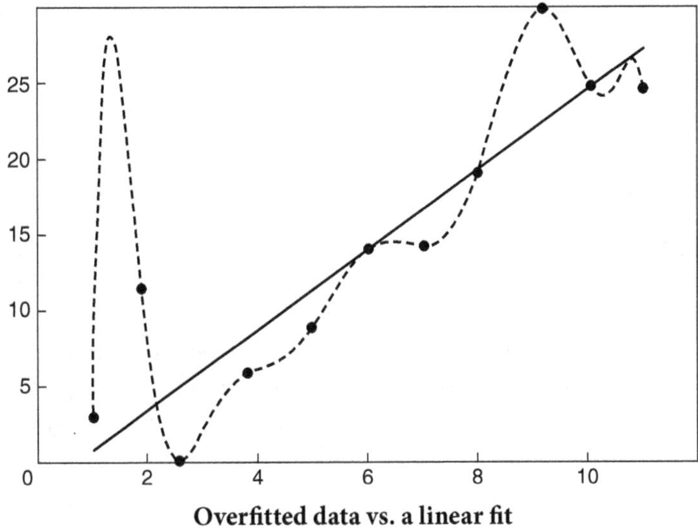

Overfitted data vs. a linear fit

The Science of Astronomy

Astronomy is the natural science that studies celestial objects and phenomena. Mathematics, physics, chemistry, and even biology are all applied to this study. Objects of study range from the contents of our solar system—including the earth and moon, the sun, the planets, and other objects such as comets and asteroids—to the farthest, largest, and oldest objects in the universe, such as exoplanets, galaxy clusters, and cosmic filaments. The evolution and fate of all of these objects are also subjects of study in astronomy, forming subdisciplines like cosmology, astrophysics, and even astrobiology.

Astronomy includes both observational and theoretical branches. *Observational astronomy* observes celestial objects and phenomena with a wide variety of instruments and techniques, while *theoretical astronomy* applies physics, mathematics, and chemistry to explain observational data and construct theoretical models of the universe.

History of Early Astronomy

Ancient Astronomy

Astronomy is probably among the earliest human scientific endeavors. Ancient people around the world have been observing the sky since at least

Neolithic times. Cultures including Mesopotamia, Egypt, Greece, Persia, India, China, and Central America all mapped the positions and motions of the stars, planets, and moon and constructed calendars. They mapped the cycles of lunar and solar eclipses and predicted the arrival of comets.

The Ptolemaic Model

The geocentric, or **Ptolemaic model**, of the solar system was named after Roman-Egyptian astronomer and mathematician **Claudius Ptolemy** (c. AD 90–168). Though he was not the first to advance an earth-centered universe as a model of the heavens, he codified and popularized it in a work that came to be called (in its later Arabic translation) the *Almagest.* It was the culmination of centuries of astronomical observation in the Mesopotamian, Egyptian, and Greco-Roman world.

The Ptolemaic model places the earth, a perfect sphere, at the center of the universe. The sun, moon, and planets move around the earth on **celestial spheres**. Each planet is moved by a system of two spheres. The first sphere, the **deferent**, moves around a point called an **eccentric**, slightly offset from the earth. This is to explain the difference in the length of the seasons (where autumn in the Northern Hemisphere is observed to be shorter than spring).

The second sphere, or **epicycle**, rotates around a point on the deferent, which in turn moves around the eccentric. The model to this point explains the **retrograde motion** observed in some planets, where they seemed to slow down, stop, or even move in reverse.

The model to this point predates Ptolemy. Ptolemy's contribution, other than codifying and describing the model, was to solve a problem with it: the model could accurately describe and predict either the location or duration of the retrograde motion of a planet, but not both at once. One way to deal with the problem is to abandon the idea of uniform circular motion of the planets. (This is, of course, the correct answer, but was not acceptable to ancient astronomers, because the heavens were thought to be perfect in the Aristotelian ideal of nature.) To solve this contradiction, Ptolemy introduced the **equant**, a point opposite the eccentric from earth's position. In the Ptolemaic model, the center of an epicycle carrying a planet must move with a constant angular speed with respect to the equant, meaning the center of the epicycle will *not* move with a constant speed along its deferent. This rule preserved uniform circular motion and allowed for a better fit to the actual observational data of the day.

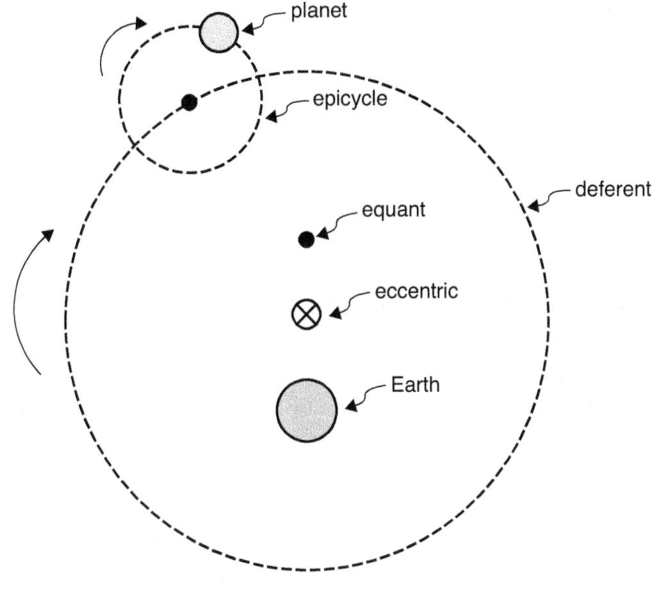

Ptolemaic model

In the Ptolemaic model, the order of the spheres outwards from Earth is: the moon, Mercury, Venus, the sun, Mars, Jupiter, Saturn, the "fixed stars," surrounded by the *Primum Mobile* (the "first moved"). Despite the complexity of its design, the Ptolemaic model provided excellent agreement with observational data.

Copernicus and the Heliocentric Model

In 1543, Polish mathematician and astronomer **Nicolaus Copernicus** published his book *De revolutionibus orbium coelestrium (On the Revolutions of the Heavenly Spheres)*, detailing a **heliocentric model** of the universe—a model that placed the sun at the center of the universe instead of the earth. Though he died shortly after its publication, this model led to the *Copernican Revolution*, often cited as the beginning of the *Scientific Revolution*.

The Copernican heliocentric model provided a practical alternative to the Ptolemaic model, proposing the following:

1. Heavenly motions are uniform, eternal, and circular or compounded of several circles (epicycles).
2. The center of the universe is near the sun.
3. Around the sun, in order, are Mercury, Venus, the earth and moon, Mars, Jupiter, Saturn, and the fixed stars.

4. The earth has three motions: daily rotation, annual revolution, and annual tilting of its axis.
5. Retrograde motion of the planets is explained by the earth's motion.
6. The distance from the earth to the sun is small compared to the distance to the stars.

Despite its differences from the Ptolemaic model—including the correct order of the planets; the correct explanation of years, days, and seasons on earth; its explanation of retrograde motion; and its observation that the "fixed stars" were much farther from the earth than the sun—the Copernican model was not more accurate in its predictions or a better fit to observational data of the time than the Ptolemaic model. Copernicus was prompted to develop his theory not by any observational results, but more by a philosophical distaste for Ptolemy's introduction of the equant, which he wanted to replace with even more epicycles. This lack of an actual scientific need for this modification, plus the way in which it removed earth from the center of the universe, led to resistance to the early adoption of the heliocentric model. It would take more observation for his model to become accepted.

Tycho Brahe and Johannes Kepler: Refining the Heliocentric Model

The additional observation was provided by **Tycho Brahe** (1546–1601), a Danish nobleman and astronomer who set a new standard for observational accuracy of stars and planets. Among his observations, he proved that novae were not objects below the orbit of the moon, thus proving that the heavens were not unchanging. In addition, he proved that comets were not atmospheric phenomena, as had been thought, but were objects that must pass through the celestial spheres, and not impervious, immutable objects. Both observations cast further doubt on the Aristotelian beliefs in an unchanging celestial realm.

Brahe's last assistant, German astronomer and mathematician **Johannes Kepler** (1571–1630), made use of Brahe's extensive collection of celestial observations to calculate the orbits of the Earth and Mars, and from there, formulate his **laws of planetary motion**. One prediction resulting from his theories (published in 1609 and 1618) was the idea that the planets did not orbit in the perfect unchanging circles of Aristotelian physics, but rather in ellipses.

The Observations of Galileo

Further empirical proof of the heliocentric model, as well as further blows to the unchanging and perfect Aristotelian heavens, were provided by the observations of **Galileo Galilei**. In 1609, Galileo built his first telescope from descriptions of similar instruments that had been recently built in Holland. He turned his new instrument to the sky and almost immediately made major discoveries.

Firstly, Galileo found that the moon, rather than being the perfect sphere demanded by Aristotelian physics, was in fact covered in mountains and craters. He was even able to estimate the height and depth of some of these lunar features from their shadows. Secondly, Galileo observed that the Milky Way was made up of many stars, with many too faint to see with the naked eye. Thirdly, he observed that Jupiter was circled by four new "planets," now called the *Galilean moons*. He tracked their orbital motion around Jupiter on consecutive nights, showing that they disappeared behind the limb of Jupiter. This provided strong evidence for the Copernican model by addressing the objection that the moon could not circle the earth, as it would get left behind in the earth's orbit around the sun. The existence of the Galilean moons showed that it was possible for objects to orbit other objects.

Later observations by Galileo included the first observation of sunspots (showing that even the sun itself was not unblemished and perfect) and, most importantly, the observation of the phases of Venus. Galileo observed that Venus had phases like the moon. In the Ptolemaic model, Venus moves on an epicycle that lies on a line between the sun and the earth at all times. This geometry means that Venus should always be seen in a crescent phase from Earth. Galileo observed a full cycle of phases from new to full and back, proving that Venus must be going around the sun. The Ptolemaic model has no way to explain that observation.

ASTROPHYSICS

Kepler's Laws and Orbits

Kepler's analysis of the observational data collected by Brahe allowed him to formulate a theoretical model of planetary orbits, resulting in what are called **Kepler's laws of planetary motion**.

Kepler's First Law

Kepler's first law states:

The orbits of the planets are ellipses with the sun at one focus.

An **ellipse** is a figure drawn around two points, called **foci**. The geometry of an ellipse can be described by two numbers. The **semi-major axis, *a***, is half the distance of the longest diameter of the ellipse.

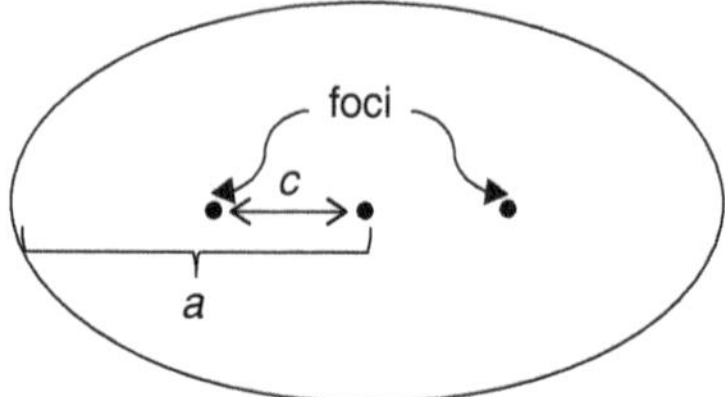

The **eccentricity, *e***, of the ellipse is half the distance between the foci (the **linear eccentricity, *c*** in the figure), divided by the semi-major axis ***a***:

$$e = \frac{c}{a}, 0 < e < 1,$$

with $e = 0$ being a circle. This eccentricity is a measure of how far from circular an ellipse is.

Kepler's Second Law: The Law of Areas

Kepler's second law, the law of areas, states:

A line from a planet to the sun sweeps over equal areas in equal intervals of time.

A necessary consequence of the law of areas is that a planet will speed up and slow down during its orbit. The extremes of a planet's orbit will also be the extremes of its orbital velocity. A planet will move fastest at its closest point to the sun, or *perihelion* (*peri-* from Greek περί- [peri-], means "near" or "closest," while *-helion* from Ηλιος [Helios], means "the sun") and slowest near its farthest point, or *aphelion* (ap- from Greek ἀπ[ό]- , ap[o]-, meaning "away from"). Together these points are the ***apsides*** of a solar orbit. In the figure illustrating Kepler's second law, note that the shaded areas are equal, as are the time intervals. Orbital velocity, however, is faster near perihelion and slower near aphelion, which demonstrates the truth of Kepler's second law.

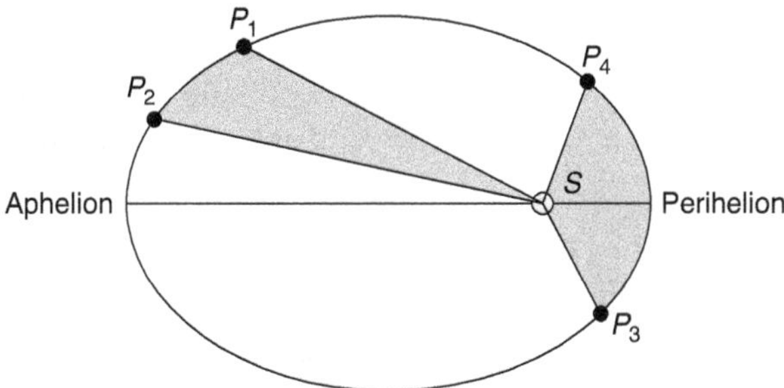

Kepler's second law: the law of areas

Kepler's Third Law: The Harmonic Law

Kepler's third law states:

The square of a planet's orbital period is proportional to the cube of the semi-major axis of its orbit.

So, in symbols, this law is $T^2 \propto a^3 \rightarrow T^2 = ka^3$, where the orbital period T is the time it takes a planet to complete its orbit and a is its semi-major axis. The variable k is equal to 1, assuming the period is expressed in units of years, and the semi-major axis is expressed in astronomical units. An **astronomical unit (AU)** is defined as earth's average distance from the sun. Since 2012, the astronomical unit has been exactly defined as one AU = 149,597,870,700 m, but a rough value of 150 million km (~93 million miles) can be used for most calculations.

Newtonian Physics and Gravity

Newton's Laws of Motion

Isaac Newton first compiled his three laws of motion in his *Philosophiæ Naturalis Principia Mathematica (Mathematical Principles of Natural Philosophy)*, published in 1687. Using these laws and his law of universal gravitation, Newton was able to explain Kepler's laws of planetary motion from a theoretical standpoint. These laws formed the basis for classical mechanics.

Important to these laws is the notion of an **inertial frame of reference**, which is defined as a frame of reference in which a body with zero net force acting upon it does not accelerate.

Newton's First Law

In an inertial frame of reference, an object either remains at rest or continues to move at a constant velocity unless acted upon by a force.

Newton's Second Law

In an inertial frame of reference, the sum of all forces on an object equals the mass of the object times the acceleration of the object.

That is to say

$$\sum \vec{F} = m\vec{a}$$

Note that this law assumes the object's mass does not change, so objects like rockets, which expel their fuel to create thrust and thus lose the mass of the fuel, require more careful consideration and something called the **rocket equation** to model.

Newton's Third Law

When one body exerts a force on a second body, the second body simultaneously exerts a force equal in magnitude and opposite in direction on the first body.

Newton's Law of Universal Gravitation

In order to explain Kepler's laws of planetary motion, Newton also needed an empirical relationship to describe the force that was causing the planets to orbit the sun. He presented a general physical law derived from empirical observation. He posited there was a force that acted instantaneously between any two masses. This force acted along the line between the two masses, and was proportional to the product of the masses. However, the force gets weaker with increasing distance, falling off as the square of the distance between the masses. Thus, **Newton's law of universal gravitation** is given by

$$F = \frac{Gm_1m_2}{r^2},$$

where F is the force of gravity between objects 1 and 2; m_1 and m_2 are the masses of the two objects; r is the distance between the two objects; and G

is a constant of proportionality called the **gravitational constant**. Gravity is actually very weak (when was the last time you were pulled toward an object that wasn't literally the size of the earth?), so the value of this constant is very small:

$$G = 6.67 \times 10^{-11}\ \text{m}^3 \cdot \text{kg}^{-1} \cdot \text{s}^{-2}.$$

Physics of Orbital Motion

With Newton's three laws of motion and the law of universal gravitation, the physics of orbital motion can be described.

An **orbit** is a gravitationally curved path of an object around another object, such as a planet around a star, or a satellite or moon around a planet. Orbits can either be **closed** (circular or elliptical), repeating over time, or **open** (parabolic or hyperbolic), one-time gravitational interactions. Generally we think of closed orbits when we use the word "orbit."

In order for an object (let's say a satellite) to orbit another massive object (such as a planet), its **tangential velocity**—its speed as it moves past the planet—must overcome the force of gravity pulling the satellite toward the center of the planet. If its tangential velocity is too low, the satellite crashes into the planet. If its velocity is high enough to break free from the planet entirely, above the **escape velocity**, the satellite sails off into space. Between those two extremes, the satellite will achieve an elliptical or circular orbit around the planet.

The simplest case is to assume a circular orbit. The acceleration needed to keep a satellite in a circular orbit is

$$a = \frac{v^2}{r},$$

where v is the satellite's speed and r the orbital radius. From Newton's second law, the inward force to overcome is

$$F = \frac{m_s v^2}{r},$$

where m_s is the mass of the satellite. Acting against this force to curve the satellite's trajectory into an orbit is the force of gravity. We can use the universal law of gravitation $F = \frac{Gm_1m_2}{r^2}$ and equate the two forces:

$$\frac{m_s v^2}{r} = \frac{G m_s m_p}{r^2},$$

where m_p is the mass of the planet. Now we can solve for v:

$$v = \sqrt{\frac{G m_p}{r}}$$

This is the satellite's **circular velocity**: how fast it is moving in a circular orbit of radius r around a planet of mass m_p.

Generalization of the Harmonic Law

Newton used his ideas to generalize Kepler's third law, the harmonic law, to any gravitational system, not just the sun and its planets:

$$T^2 = \left(\frac{4\pi^2}{G}\right)\left(\frac{a^3}{m_1 + m_2}\right),$$

where T is the orbital period, a is the semi-major axis of the orbit, and $m_1 + m_2$ is the combined masses of the objects.

Conserved Quantities

Another concept in physics that is important in astronomy is that of **conserved quantities**. These are quantities whose values remain constant in a system over time. Many physical laws express some sort of conservation, but most important for the current discussion are **conservation of energy**, **conservation of momentum**, and **conservation of angular momentum**.

Energy is conserved in a system, with no energy being created or destroyed. In fact, all the energy (and mass; we'll see they are interchangeable) in the universe has been here since the beginning.

Linear momentum is the product of an object's mass times its velocity. In any inertial frame of reference it is a conserved quantity.

Angular momentum is the rotational equivalent of linear momentum, depending not only on the mass and the velocity but also on the distance of the mass from the center of rotation. It too is conserved in a closed system.

All three of these conserved quantities will prove important in the study of astronomy.

Relativity

In 1905, **Albert Einstein** published a paper outlining his theory of special relativity. Together with his theory of general relativity in 1915, Einstein's theories revolutionized physics, including the field of astronomy.

Special Relativity

The **theory of special relativity** was prompted by Einstein thinking about how moving observers would see events around them. The 1905 paper, *On the Electrodynamics of Moving Bodies*, shows that Einstein was thinking especially about light, an electromagnetic phenomenon. His conclusions led to several postulates with far-reaching consequences.

First Postulate—the principle of relativity:

> **The laws of physics are the same for all observers in uniform motion relative to one another.**

Uniform motion here refers to motion that is not accelerated—an "inertial frame of reference." Consider sitting in a motionless spaceship in deep space, when along comes another spaceship moving uniformly toward you. Or is it? An observer in that other ship might just as well conclude that they are motionless, and you are the one moving. An observer between the ships might conclude that *both* ships are moving. There is no experiment or observation that can be done to determine which observer is right. That is because it all is relative to the observer. There exists no fixed frame of reference from which to measure, a large departure from the ideas of Newtonian mechanics.

Second Postulate—the speed of light:

> **The speed of light in a vacuum is constant, with the same value for all observers independent of their motion relative to the light source.**

This is a requirement of the first postulate, otherwise all that the observers in the spaceships would have to do is measure the speed of light in their ship and thus determine who is moving.

Consequences of Special Relativity

The postulates of special relativity have several important consequences:

1. **Relativity of simultaneity:** Two events that are simultaneous for one observer may not be simultaneous for another observer in relative uniform motion.
2. **Time dilation:** Observers at rest in their frame of reference will observe a moving clock to tick more slowly than their own "stationary" clock.
3. **Length contraction:** Objects that are moving with respect to the observer will appear to be shortened in the direction of their motion.
4. **The speed of light is a universal limit:** No physical object, signal, or effect can travel faster than the speed of light in a vacuum.
   - This includes the effect of gravity, unlike Newton's theory that gravity acts instantaneously.
5. **Mass-energy equivalence:** Mass and energy are equivalent and transmutable.
   - Famously expressed as $E = mc^2$, where c is the speed of light in a vacuum.
   - Thus, objects acquire more mass as they increase in energy, adding **relativistic mass** on top of their **rest mass.**
   - Also, even massless objects like photons can have momentum: $E = pc$, where p is momentum.

General Relativity

Einstein developed his theory of general relativity between 1907 and 1915 in order to incorporate gravity into his new theories. Special relativity deals exclusively with uniform motion, under which objects are not accelerating. Einstein proposed a thought experiment: Consider an observer in a closed room. The observer drops a ball, and the ball falls. There is no way for the observer to determine if the room is at rest in a gravitational field, such as sitting on the surface of the earth, or if the room is in a rocket far from any massive object, being accelerated at 9.8 m/s^2, equal to earth's gravitational acceleration.

This insight led to the **equivalence principle:**

Observers cannot distinguish between inertial forces due to acceleration and uniform gravitational forces due to the presence of a massive body.

An object of mass m accelerated by an inertial force, like a rocket, feels a force due to Newton's second law. That same object of mass m near a large object, like a planet of mass M, feels a force due to gravity of $F_{gravity} = \frac{GMm}{r^2}$

by Newton's law of gravitation. The equivalence principle means that the *m* in the first equation and the *m* in the second are the same quantity—that the thing that resists acceleration is the same thing that feels the force of gravity, which might seem obvious, but is actually profound.

From this point, Einstein developed a theory of gravity that fit with special relativity. Space and time are bound together in a single four-dimensional entity called **space-time**. Mass causes local space-time to curve. In turn, objects follow the shortest path in this curved space-time, which is called a **geodesic**. Far from any mass, this will be a straight line, but near a massive object, like a planet or star, that line will begin to curve, and the object will be accelerated toward the massive object.

Gravity according to General Relativity:

Mass tells space-time how to curve, and the curvature of space-time tells mass how to accelerate.

Thus, in general relativity, gravitational acceleration is not an instantaneous force between objects, but a natural consequence of the curvature of space-time caused by the presence of mass.

Consequences of General Relativity

Consequences of this space-time curvature include:

1. **Gravitational time dilation:** Clocks run slower in deeper gravitational wells.
2. **Light deflection:** The path of light is bent by the presence of a mass, called **gravitational lensing**.
3. **Orbital precession differences:** The orbit of Mercury **precesses**, meaning that its aphelion position does not repeat, but moves around the sun in a circle. This precession is faster than can be explained by Newtonian gravity.
4. **Frame dragging:** Rotating massive objects drag space-time along with them.
5. **Expansion of space:** The universe is expanding, as will be covered later, and the farther away space is, the faster it is moving away—a consequence of space-time itself expanding.

CELESTIAL SYSTEMS

Celestial Motions

The Celestial Sphere

Ancient astronomers perceived the sky as a giant sphere, with the stars fixed on it and the planets, sun, and moon between the earth and this sphere. They grouped the stars into **constellations** and named those shapes after heroes and gods. Though we now know the stars are at varying distances, all far from the solar system, it is still useful for observational purposes to think of the stars as a **celestial sphere** on which celestial phenomena sit.

The celestial sphere appears to rotate westward around the earth each day due to the eastward rotation of the earth. From any location on the earth's surface only half of the celestial sphere will be visible. The point on the celestial sphere directly above the head of an observer is called the **zenith**, while the point on the celestial sphere directly below the observer (and thus hidden by the earth) is called the **nadir**.

The Celestial Coordinate System

The position of celestial objects can be located on the celestial sphere using the **celestial coordinate system**. This is analogous to the coordinate system of latitude and longitude used on the earth's surface, but projected onto the inside surface of a sphere. The point directly above the North Pole in the extension of earth's axis of rotation intersecting the celestial sphere is the **celestial north pole**, while the point directly below the South Pole in the extension of earth's axis of rotation intersecting the celestial sphere is the **celestial south pole**. The celestial sphere is divided into northern and southern hemispheres by the **celestial equator**. Located near the celestial north pole is the star Polaris, the "North Star."

Because the earth's axis of rotation is tilted with respect to its orbital plane at an angle of 23.5°, the path of the sun through the sky—the **ecliptic**—does not follow the celestial equator, but is instead inclined by the same 23.5°. The sun spends half of the year above the celestial equator in the northern celestial hemisphere and half below in the southern celestial hemisphere. The sun crosses the celestial equator from south to north on the **vernal equinox**, which typically occurs on March 21, and from north to south on the **autumnal equinox**, typically September 22. On these days the lengths of day and night are equal (thus *equinox*, Latin for "equal night"). For observers in the Northern Hemisphere, the points when the sun is farthest north and south of the celestial equator are the **summer solstice** (June 22) and **winter solstice** (December 22), respectively. The term *solstice* means "stand still," as the sun appears to stand still with respect to its apparent north–south drift on the celestial sphere at that time. As the sun travels along the ecliptic, it crosses 13 constellations. These constellations are known as the **zodiac constellations**, and the **zodiac** is a band of stars centered around the ecliptic that includes these 13 constellations.

The celestial equivalent of latitude is called **declination (Dec)**, measured in degrees from the celestial equator, $0^\circ < \text{Dec} \leq +90^\circ$ in the northern celestial hemisphere and $-90^\circ \leq \text{Dec} < 0^\circ$ in the southern celestial hemisphere, with the celestial equator at $\text{Dec} = 0^\circ$.

The celestial equivalent of longitude is called **right ascension (RA)**. RA could easily be measured in degrees, but it is more customary to measure RA in hours (h), minutes (m) and seconds (s) of arc, with 24^h being equivalent to a full circle. This is because astronomers can then measure a star's location by timing its passage through the highest point in the sky as the earth rotates. RA is measured from the point on the celestial equator where the sun passes through going south to north on the vernal equinox, called the **First Point of Aries**, at $\text{RA} = 0^h$. Since there are 360 degrees in a circle and 24 hours in a day, 1^h of right ascension is equivalent to 15° of apparent sky rotation.

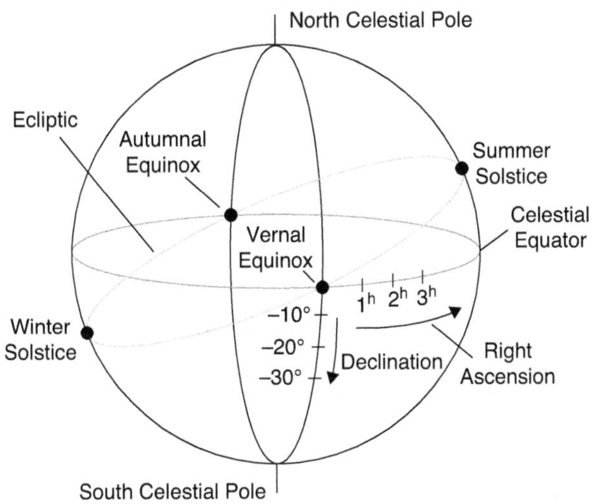

The celestial coordinate system

Short- and Long-Term Motion in the Celestial Sphere

The position of stars in the celestial sphere isn't perfectly fixed over the course of the year. As the earth moves though its orbit, the position of the earth changes with respect to stars, a phenomenon known as **parallax**. The earth is on opposite sides of the sun every six months, so observing a star at this interval gives the largest parallax angle, the **annual parallax**. The **parsec (pc)** is a unit defined as the distance of an object for which the annual parallax is one arcsecond, and corresponds to 3.26 light years.

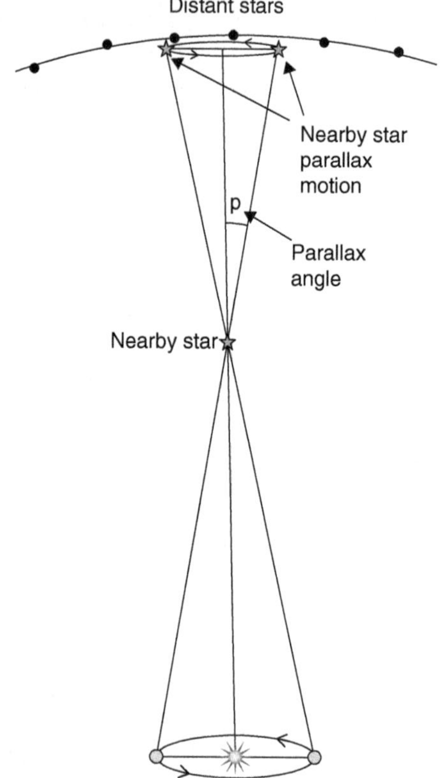

Annual parallax

The figure above is exaggerated, as even the nearby stars exhibit very small parallax angles, but measuring parallax is still a useful tool for establishing distances for nearby stars. The closest star, Proxima Centauri, has an annual parallax of 0.7687 ± 0.003 arcseconds, at a distance of about 4.244 light years (1.301 pc). The fact that parallax angles are so small that they were basically unobservable in ancient times led early astronomers to argue against the heliocentric model. The enormous sizes required to render stellar parallax unobservable seemed preposterous to early astronomers.

The First Point of Aries isn't actually currently in the constellation Aries at this epoch. This is because the celestial poles and the celestial equator slowly shift their positions due to the motion of the earth's axis of rotation, called **precession**. If the earth were a perfect sphere, its axis of rotation would remain fixed with respect to the sky. However, the earth bulges at the equator due to its rotation, leading to its axis of rotation being dragged in a circle, like a wobbling top, over the course of thousands of years. A full precession cycle take's around 26,000 years to return "celestial north" to the same position.

Apparent Magnitude

How can the brightness of two different stars be compared? Ancient astronomers, such as the Greek astronomer Hipparchus (160–130 BC), classified the visible stars into six groups by brightness, called **apparent magnitude**. The brightest stars were first magnitude, and the next dimmer, second magnitude, and so on down to the sixth magnitude. Later astronomers noted that each magnitude was about 2.5 times brighter than the next dimmer magnitude, and that a first magnitude star was about 100 times brighter than a sixth magnitude star. This system was extended and made quantitative by Oxford astronomer **Norman Pogson** in 1854, who defined **Pogson's ratio**:

The brightness ratio between two stars whose apparent magnitude differs by one magnitude is 2.512.

To calculate apparent magnitude, the following formula can be used, with R being the ratio of the brightnesses of the two objects and Δm being the difference in their apparent magnitudes:

$$R = 2.512^{\Delta m} \text{ or } \Delta m = 2.512 \times \log_{10} R$$

This allows stars to have an exact number for reference, and extends that number below 0 and above 6. Sirius, the brightest star in our sky, has an apparent magnitude of −1.46, while the planet Venus has a magnitude of −4.2. Very faint visible stars have apparent magnitudes around +6.5.

This scale needs a reference brightness for its zero point. Pogson chose Polaris, the North Star; however, later observation showed that Polaris is a **variable star**, with changing brightness, so the star Vega was chosen. The modern magnitude scale uses a more complex reference method, but Vega is still magnitude 0.

This scale says nothing about the actual brightness of the star or object—just how it appears in the night sky on earth.

Earth and the Moon

The Moon's Orbit

The moon completes its eastward orbit around the earth in 27.3 days, an interval known as the moon's **sidereal period**. The moon's orbit is slightly inclined from the earth's ecliptic plane—about 5 degrees. The moon is in a **synchronous orbit** around the earth, meaning its period of rotation (the moon's "day") is nearly equal to its sidereal period. This means that it keeps one face toward the earth at all times—the **near side of the moon**—and one side pointed permanently away from the earth—the so-called **far side** or **dark side of the moon**. The "dark" side of the moon is, of course, not actually dark. It receives light from the sun just like the near side during its day-night cycle, but it is not viewable from the earth's surface. In fact, only 59% of the moon's surface is viewable from earth due to apparent "wagging" in the moon's orbital motion known as **libration**.

Phases of the Moon

As the moon orbits around the earth, the half of the moon that faces the sun will be lit. A changing portion of that lit face will be visible from earth, known as the **phases of the moon**. These are divided into eight major phases:

- New moon
- Waxing crescent moon
- First quarter moon
- Waxing gibbous moon
- Full moon
- Waning gibbous moon
- Last quarter moon
- Waning crescent moon

The cycle of the moon's phases repeats every 29.5 days, known as the moon's **synodic period**.

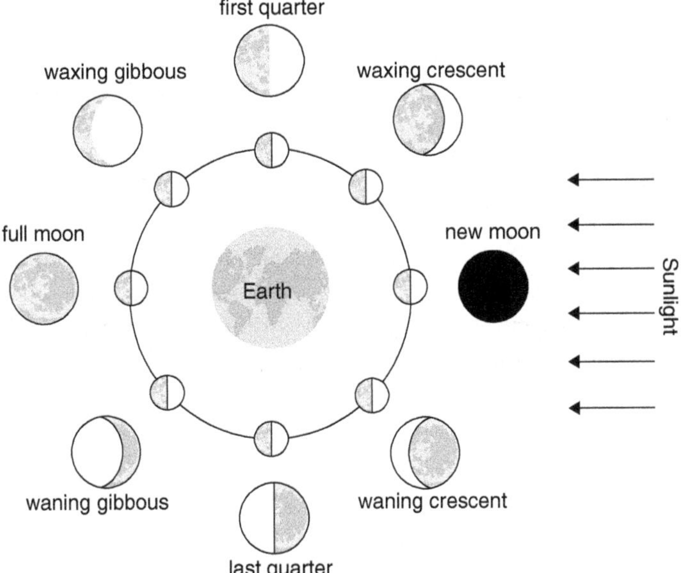

The phases of the moon as seen in the Northern Hemisphere

The Moon and the Tides

The gravitational pull of the moon on the earth pulls the earth toward it, causing a bulge on both sides of the earth along the line joining the earth and the moon. These **tidal forces** affect the earth's crust to some extent, but have a much larger and more noticeable effect on earth's oceans, causing the **tides**. There are two high and two low tides every 24 hours as a result. Since the moon is orbiting in the direction of the earth's rotation, high tides occur about every 12 hours and 25 minutes; the extra 25 minutes are due to the moon's orbit.

The sun also has a tidal effect on the earth's oceans. When the sun, moon, and earth are lined up with the sun's gravitational pull, reinforcing that of the moon (a conjunction called a **syzygy**), a tidal *maximum* called a **spring tide** occurs. This happens about twice a month around the time of the full and new moons. When the moon is in the first or third quarter, the sun and the moon are 90° apart, causing a tidal *minimum* known as a **neap tide**.

The effect of the tidal forces on the earth's crust are less easy to see, but they are responsible for slowing the rotation of the earth and the moon over time, leading to the moon's synchronous orbit. This interaction transfers angular momentum to the moon, lowering its orbital speed and increasing its orbital distance over time. The moon's mean orbital distance increases by about 38 mm a year, and the earth's day increases by about 15 microseconds a year, both due to the moon's tidal forces at work.

Lagrange Points of the Earth–Moon System

The **Lagrange points** are named for **Joseph-Louis Lagrange**, the Italian mathematician and astronomer who, along with Leonhard Euler, predicted and described them. The five points (L1 through L5) are shown below. These are points in the earth–moon system where the gravitational pull of the earth is balanced by that of the moon.

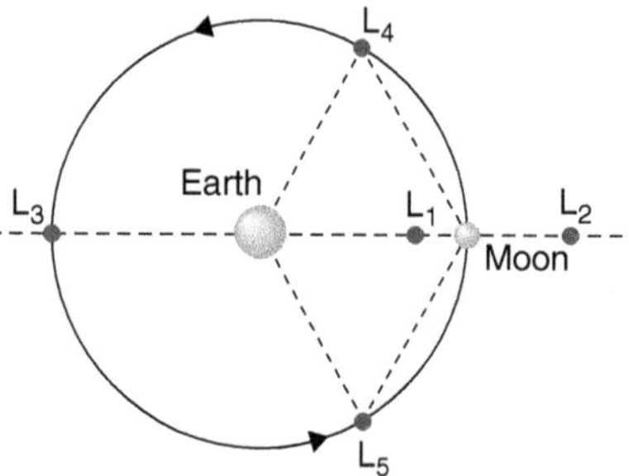

The Earth–Moon Lagrange points

There are Lagrange points in any system of two massive objects, not just the earth–moon system. Not all Lagrange points are stable, though there can still be stable orbits that keep objects near them. An object that orbits near the L4 or L5 points (ahead or behind the course of its orbit) are called Trojan satellites, so those points are sometimes called Trojan points. Jupiter has large clusters of asteroids at its L4 and L5 solar Lagrange points, the "Greek camp" and "Trojan camp," respectively, named after characters from the Iliad.

Solar and Lunar Eclipses

A **solar eclipse** occurs when the moon passes between the earth and the sun, blocking the sun's light from hitting the earth (a *syzygy*). This occurs during a new moon, as the lit side of the moon is obviously facing away from the earth. Due to differences in the apparent size of the sun and moon (a consequence of non-circular orbits), solar eclipses are sometimes **total**, with the sun completely blocked, or **annular**, with a ring of sun visible around the moon.

A **lunar eclipse** occurs when the earth blocks the sun's light hitting the moon (the other type of syzygy possible). This can occur during a full moon, as the lit side of the moon is facing the earth at this point. The moon is not completely black during a lunar eclipse, as sunlight refracted by the earth's atmosphere still illuminates the lunar surface. However, the refracted light is less than full sunlight and is red as a consequence of **Rayleigh scattering** of the blue light in the atmosphere, causing the moon to appear dimmer and redder than normal.

An eclipse does not occur at every syzygy because of the ~5° inclination of the moon's orbit from the earth's ecliptic. This prevents perfect alignment during every twice-monthly conjunction. Instead, solar and lunar eclipses occur on an 18-year cycle called a **saros**.

Seasons, Calendars, and Timekeeping

Tropical vs. Sidereal Year

The current calendar, called the **Gregorian calendar**, is based on the **tropical year**, a period 365.242199 solar days long. A **solar day** is the 24-hour period it takes for the earth's rotation to return the sun to the same local meridian. Though we start the calendar year on January 1 in common usage, the tropical year actually measures the time from one vernal equinox to the following one, or from the start of one spring to the next. This period of one year is a complete orbit of the earth around the sun. The tropical year is not an integer number of days, being about a quarter of a day longer than 365. This requires the insertion of a leap year of 366 days every four calendar years to keep the Gregorian calendar in line with the tropical year.

If, instead of measuring days by the sun, you measured the period it took a given star to complete its rotation around the sky and return to the same position, you would get a period of 23h, 56m, and 4.09s, somewhat shorter than a 24-hour solar day. This period is called a **sidereal day**, and 366 of these sidereal days make up a **sidereal year**, corresponding to the ~365+1 rotations of the earth during that period. During this period the sun completes one apparent rotation around the celestial sphere along the ecliptic.

Lunar Months and the Lunar Calendar

The synodic lunar period—the time from new moon to new moon or full moon to full moon—is 29.5 days long. This easily observed and measured period was the basis for many ancient calendars around the world (and is still the basis for many religious calendars, such as the Islamic and Jewish calendars). However, this synodic period, or **lunar month**, is not an integer number of days, and the Gregorian calendar does not divide evenly into lunar months (there are ~12.37 lunar months in a solar year), so the **lunar calendar** will not stay in synch with the seasons over time. Nevertheless, the lunar cycle is used to calculate eclipse cycles.

Axial Tilt and the Seasons

If the earth's axis of rotation was not inclined with respect to the direction of its orbit, a given latitude on the earth's surface would receive exactly the same amount of sunlight throughout the year, as the equator does now. Higher and lower latitudes would be cooler than near the equator, but there would be no seasonal variation.

Instead, the earth's axis of rotation is inclined at an angle of 23.5°. Due to the **axial tilt**, latitudes north and south of the equator experience a variation in the amount of incident sunlight over the course of the year, causing the seasons. During the period, when a hemisphere is inclined toward the sun, it experiences summer, and during the period it is tilted away, it experiences winter. Since inclining one hemisphere toward the sun inclines the other hemisphere away, the Northern Hemisphere and the Southern Hemisphere experience opposite seasons—the northern summer is the southern winter and vice versa.

It might be a reasonable assumption to conclude that the position of the earth in its orbit might have some effect on how much incident sunlight the earth receives, but in fact, the difference between perihelion and aphelion is not significant to the amount of sunlight incident on the earth. In fact, northern summer is closer to the earth's aphelion than its perihelion.

THE SCIENCE OF LIGHT

The Electromagnetic Spectrum

Light as a Particle and a Wave

Scientists from ancient times on through the late nineteenth and early twentieth centuries debated the nature of light—whether light was a **wave** (i.e., an oscillation in some medium) or a **particle** (a discrete packet of energy). Work in the mid-nineteenth century on the physics of electromagnetism clearly showed that light was an electromagnetic wave. Differing colors of visible light, plus the other types of electromagnetic radiation then known, such as ultraviolet and infrared light, were just waves of differing frequencies forming an **electromagnetic spectrum**.

This did not settle matters, however. There existed physical phenomena, such as the photoelectric effect, that were better explained if light were a particle, with each particle having energy and momentum. Further, work by Max Planck with blackbody radiation (discussed below) showed that electromagnetic radiation was required to be **quantized**—that is to say portioned out in discrete packets of minimum allowable energy. These light particles, called **photons**, served as these EM quanta. These are massless particles that convey electromagnetic energy.

The conclusion we have today is that the nature of light cannot be adequately described by either the wave picture or the particle picture alone, but the actual nature of light shares elements of both, and that evidence of both can be found depending on the nature of the observation or experiment. This is called the **wave–particle duality** of EM radiation.

The Mechanics of EM Waves and Photons

Waves are a periodic oscillation, which is to say that the same number of wave peaks pass a certain point in a certain time period. This is called the wave's **frequency** f, and it is measured in units of Hertz (Hz), which have a dimension of inverse seconds (s^{-1}). Related to the frequency of a wave is its **wavelength** λ—the distance from one wave peak to another, measured in meters (m). The distance from the highest point to the equilibrium position of a wave over a single period is its **amplitude**, which may vary over time. The speed of all electromagnetic (EM) radiation in a vacuum is the speed of light in a vacuum, c, which has an exactly defined value in SI units of $c = 299792485 \text{ m/s} \approx 3.00 \times 10^8 \text{ m/s}$.

The wavelength and frequency of a wave are related by

$$f = \frac{c}{\lambda}.$$

The **energy of an electromagnetic wave** (or photon) is given by

$$E = hf = \frac{hc}{\lambda},$$

where the constant $h = 6.62607015 \times 10^{-34}\,\mathrm{J \cdot s}$ is called **Planck's constant.** Thus energy is quantized in units of h. The **momentum of a photon** is given by

$$p = \frac{E}{c} = \frac{hf}{c} = \frac{h}{\lambda}$$

The Electromagnetic (EM) Spectrum

Electromagnetic waves can be arranged in an **electromagnetic (EM) spectrum** from high-energy/high-frequency/short-wavelength EM radiation, such as gamma and X-rays, through ultraviolet, visible light, and infrared light, to low-energy/low-frequency/long-wavelength EM radiation like microwaves and radio waves.

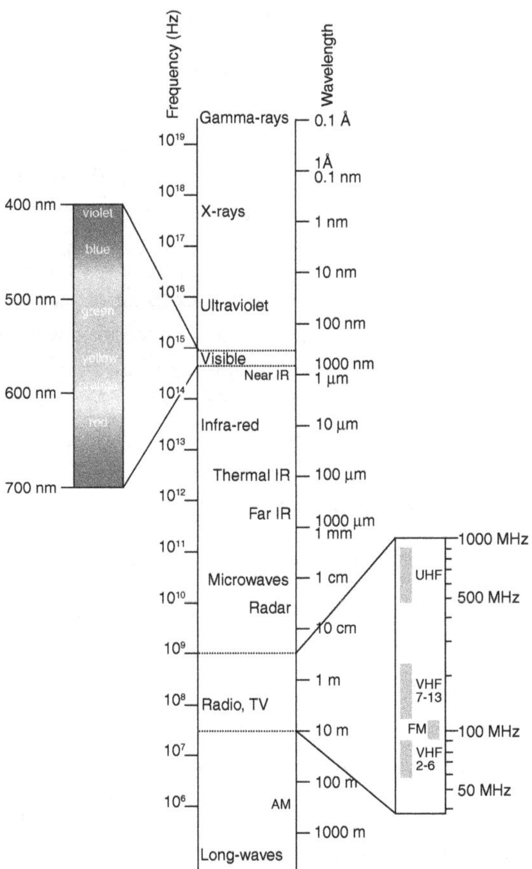

The electromagnetic spectrum, with visible light and radio wave bands highlighted

The EM spectrum covers a huge range of wavelengths/frequencies/energies. As can be seen from the figure, **visible light**, the light our eyes can perceive, makes up only a small portion of the EM spectrum—about 400–700 nm wavelengths. Immediately shorter in wavelength is **ultraviolet (UV) radiation**, and above that, **X-rays** and **gamma rays**, all of which are energetic enough to harm living things. On the longer wavelength side of visible light is **infrared (IR) radiation**, followed by **microwaves** and increasingly longer-wavelength **radio waves**.

The Doppler Effect: Blueshift and Redshift

The **Doppler effect** is the change in frequency or wavelength of a wave in relation to an observer who is moving relative to the wave source. It is named after Austrian physicist **Christian Doppler**, who described this effect in 1842. An everyday example of this effect is the sound a car makes as it approaches you, the pitch of the car noise rising until it goes past you, and the pitch of the noise dropping as it pulls away from you.

When an object emitting waves moves closer to an observer, the observed waves will decrease in wavelength as each successive wave crest arrives earlier than the one before. This corresponds to an increase in frequency as more wave peaks arrive at the observer in a given period. This will mean the object's radiation will shift toward the blue end of the spectrum, a phenomenon called **blueshift**. If the object is moving away, the radiation it emits will conversely experience **redshift**.

Light from objects moving toward the observer is *blueshifted*.

Light from objects moving away from the observer is *redshifted*.

Telescopes and the Measurement of Light

Characteristics of Telescopes

Regardless of type, all telescopes share certain characteristics and limitations. Telescopes gather EM radiation over a range of wavelengths (visible light, X-ray, UV, IR, and even radio) determined by the details of their construction and detectors. Telescopes all have a **light-gathering power** that is directly related to its **collecting area**, the total area that is capable of gathering radiation: the larger the telescope, the fainter a radiation source it is able to observe. Telescopes are limited in their **angular resolution**: the smallest angular size object for which they can form a distinct, separate image. One important thing that determines resolution of a telescope is the **diffraction limit**. Incoming EM waves are subject to **diffraction**, where they are bent by their interaction with the telescope lens(es) or detectors, causing them to spread out and limit the smallest-sized object that can be resolved. Diffraction is wavelength-dependent. For a circular mirror with otherwise perfect optical components we can write a limit as shown (where D is the telescope's diameter):

$$\theta(\text{arcsec}) = 2.06 \times 10^5 \frac{\lambda}{D},$$

Optical telescopes face other challenges. The fact that the **refraction of light**—how the path of light is bent in a medium—is wavelength-dependent means that different wavelengths, when traversing the same lens, will be refracted differently: red light will be bent the least and blue light the most. This leads to a distortion of the image formed by the telescope called **chromatic aberration**, which must be corrected for and taken into account during telescope design.

Types of Optical Telescopes

Optical telescopes come in two basic types: refracting telescopes and reflecting telescopes. A **refracting telescope** uses a lens to gather and concentrate incoming light. Light is refracted (bent) by the **objective lens** when passing through a **focus**, then gathered and made parallel again by a **secondary lens** or eyepiece to form an image on the detector (or eye). As seen above, reflecting telescopes will suffer from chromatic aberration unless the lens is designed to be more complex (and heavier and more expensive). Isaac Newton designed the first **reflecting telescope**, in which a *primary mirror* is placed at the bottom of a tube, and a flat *secondary mirror* is placed above the tube near the focus, which directs light to the objective lens and detector. Other designs of reflecting telescope are in use, such as the Cassegrain design, but all use mirrors instead of lenses.

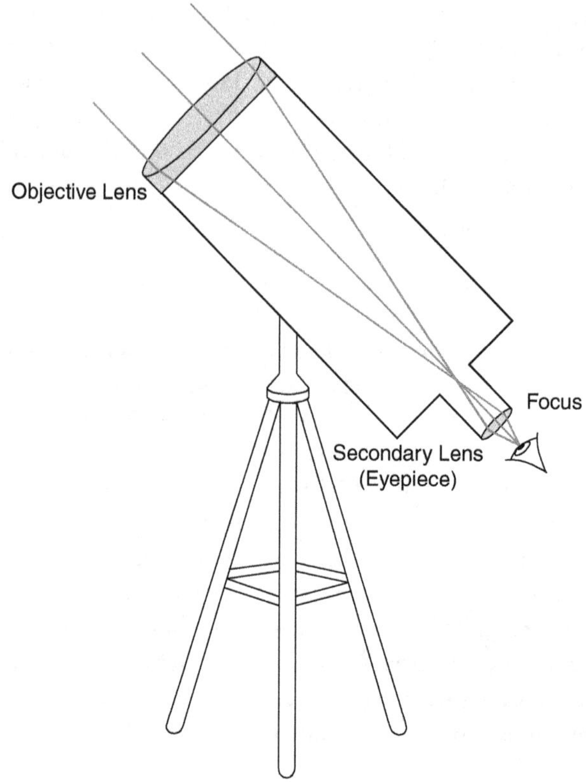

A refracting telescope

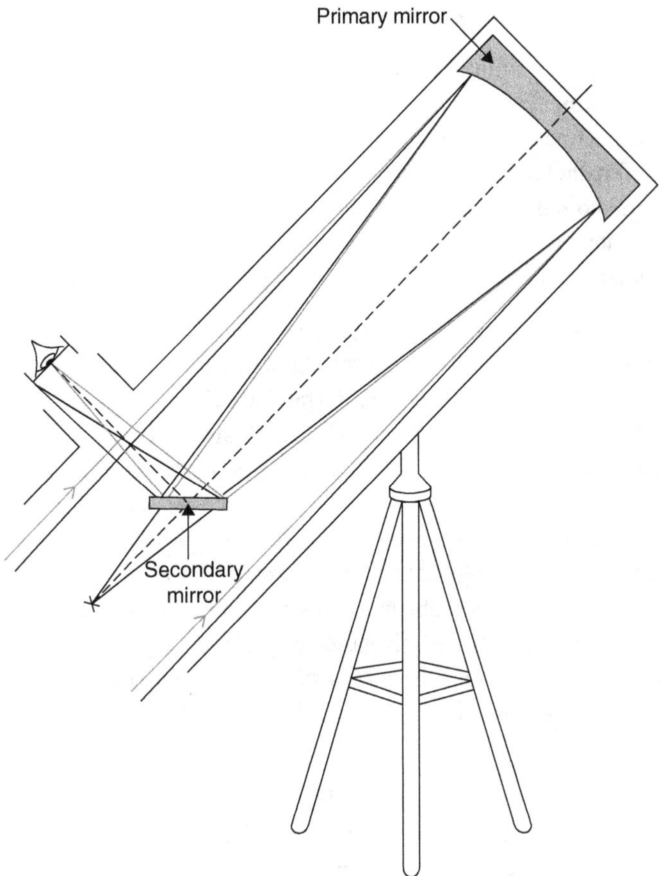

A Newtonian reflecting telescope

In both reflecting and refracting telescopes, the distance from the primary lens or mirror to the focus is called the **focal length**.

Reflecting telescopes have many advantages over refracting telescopes:

1. Reflecting telescopes do not suffer from chromatic aberration as the light is reflected instead of refracted.
2. Telescope mirrors are much lighter than than lenses of equal size.
3. Reflecting telescopes can be made much shorter for a given focal length than refracting telescopes due to their secondary mirror.

Despite the above advantages, reflecting telescopes were used into the twentieth century as scientific instruments because of the difficulty and expense of making precise telescope mirrors.

IR, UV, and Radio Telescopes

Telescopes can be built to collect EM radiation outside of the visible spectrum. Instruments are in use to probe the UV, IR, X-ray, and radio bands. **Radio telescopes** consist of arrays of instruments linked together to form an **interferometer**, a device that takes the signal from two or more instruments and combines them to produce an image. The distance between two instruments, rather than their individual sizes, will determine the angular resolution of an interferometric array, so such arrays are often very large.

Wavelengths outside of the visible spectrum interact with the earth's atmosphere differently from visible light. As will be discussed in the section on spectroscopy, materials absorb certain wavelengths of radiation while remaining transparent to others. The earth's atmosphere is no exception. UV radiation is blocked by the atmosphere's ozone layer, and the abundant water vapor in the atmosphere blocks IR wavelengths. Even visible light is distorted by the atmosphere, causing the stars to twinkle. Scientific instruments are often placed in very dry areas and/or on top of mountains to avoid as much of this problem as possible. Some smaller instruments are flown on specially outfitted airplanes to get even higher. The best possible view comes from space-based instruments in earth or even solar orbit, above the atmosphere entirely, such as the Hubble Space Telescope and the Chandra X-ray Observatory.

Space-based instruments are expensive and difficult to modify or fix, and ground-based instruments can be made much larger. To mitigate the problem of atmospheric distortion, corrections such as **adaptive optics** are used, in which a very flexible telescope mirror is deformed in real time based on the behavior of a reference laser directed into the atmosphere along the intended path of observation.

Spectroscopy

Spectroscopy uses radiation to study the elemental composition of celestial objects. Astronomers can't generally study such objects up close, and therefore need to rely on a technique that works from far away.

Excitation of Atoms

The electrons that make up the outer shell of atoms can only have certain, quantized energies, called **energy levels**. Further, an atom can only interact with radiation that will cause a transition from one of these allowed energy levels to another. When an atom interacts with an incident photon of the right wavelength, it excites an electron from the atom's **ground state** to an **excited state**. Such a state is generally unstable, and the electron returns to its ground state or another open lower energy state. This requires that it emits a photon of energy equal to the energy difference between the initial excited state and the final state.

Absorption and Emission Spectra

These differences in energy states are like fingerprints for the atom, giving a unique pattern of absorbed and emitted energies called a **spectrum**. An **absorption spectrum** results when radiation passes through a cool gas. Atoms in the gas absorb certain wavelengths, which are then missing from the radiation, and appear as dark lines in the spectrum of the radiation. The position of these lines is unique to the elemental composition of the gas.

An **emission spectrum** is produced from photons emitted by an excited gas. Only those lines corresponding to the transitions from the atoms in the excited gas are seen, appearing as bright lines. Again, the position of these lines is unique to the elemental composition of the gas.

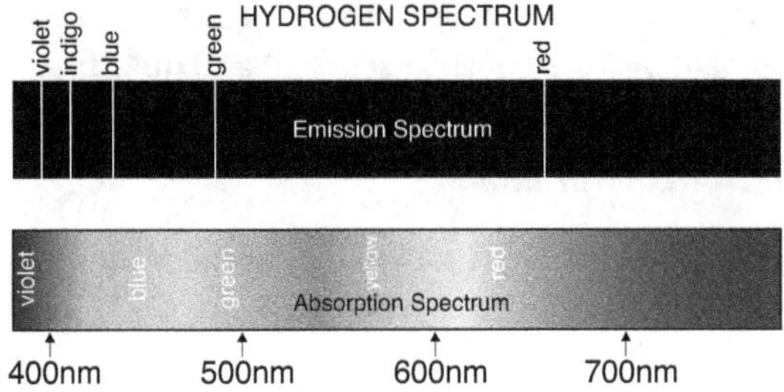

The emission and absorption spectra of hydrogen

Blackbody Radiation

Spectrum of a Heated Object

But what about the spectrum from a dense gas of solid or liquid bulk mass? Such a mass will produce a **continuous spectrum** when heated or excited, radiating in all wavelengths. This spectrum from a heated object will not have equal intensity at all wavelengths, however. Neither will it remain unchanging as the object changes temperature.

The continuous spectrum of radiation from a heated object is known as **blackbody radiation.** A **blackbody** is a theoretical object that is a perfect absorber and emitter of radiation, a cavity where the walls absorb and emit all light, sampled from a tiny slit in one of the walls. Such an object would appear black at room temperature, thus its name, but would glow at shorter and shorter wavelengths as it was heated. Though no real object is a blackbody, real objects actually are pretty close, as most of the emission of radiation from their atoms is reabsorbed internally, and only radiation emitted at the surface escapes.

The "Ultraviolet Catastrophe" and Quantization

Scientists studied this system throughout the nineteenth century. Work by Max Planck to determine the shape of the graph of intensity versus wavelength for a blackbody at different temperatures led to a problem: if radiation waves emitted by the blackbody are permitted to be any arbitrary energy, the graph of intensity would quickly diverge to infinity near the UV portion of the blackbody spectrum, a problem called the **ultraviolet catastrophe.** Planck's solution was to propose that energy could not assume an arbitrary intensity, but was instead quantized into discrete packets. Planck's proposal was the basis upon which Einstein developed the concept of photons (previously discussed) and **quantum mechanics.**

The Stefan–Boltzmann Law

Quantizing the energy resulted in a relation of intensity versus wavelength that did not diverge to infinity, shown in the figure. This curve changes with temperature, shifting the peak of the spectrum and the total energy. The total energy emitted is proportional to the total area under the curve, and is given by the **Stefan–Boltzmann** law (for a given temperature T in Kelvin): $E = \sigma T^4$, where $\sigma = 5.67 \times 10^{-8}\ \mathrm{W \cdot m^{-2} \cdot K^{-4}}$ is the **Stefan–Boltzmann constant.** This total energy is also known as the **radiant emittance.**

Wein's Law

The peak wavelength λ_{max} of the blackbody radiation spectrum for a given temperature T in Kelvin is given by **Wein's law:**

$$\lambda_{max} = \frac{b}{T}.$$

The constant of proportionality $b \cong 2.90 \times 10^{-3}\ \text{m} \cdot \text{K}$ is called **Wein's displacement constant**. Therefore, *increasing the temperature of an object causes the peak wavelength it emits to shift lower*, and the object begins to glow red, then orange, then yellow, all the way through to blue and violet.

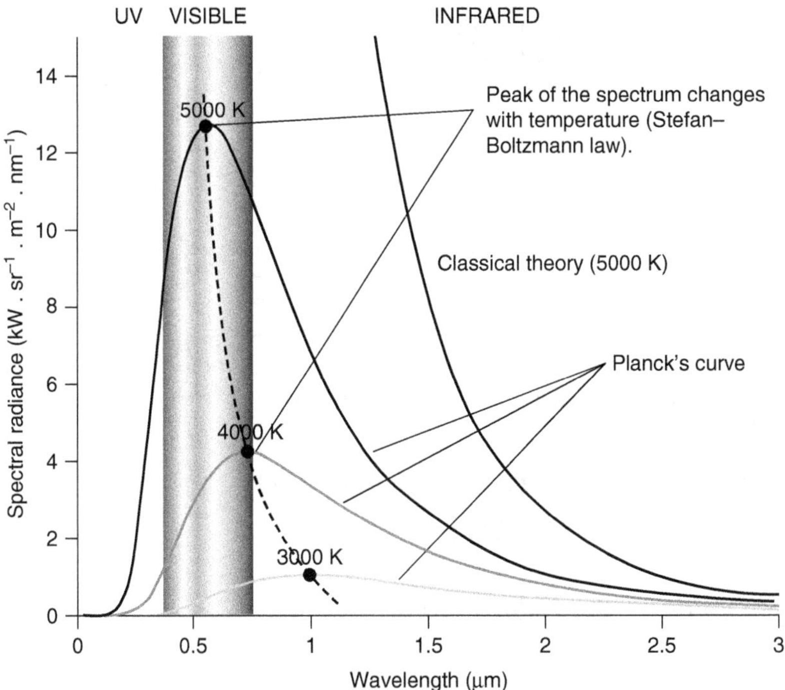

Blackbody radiation at different temperatures (The classical physics prediction is also shown.)

Luminosity vs. Brightness

Luminosity refers to the amount of light leaving a source per unit of time. **Brightness**, on the other hand, refers to the amount of light striking a given area per unit of time. Brightness b therefore depends not only on the luminosity L of the source, but also the area over which that energy is spread, and thus the distance r from the source *squared*:

$$b = \frac{L}{4\pi r^2}$$

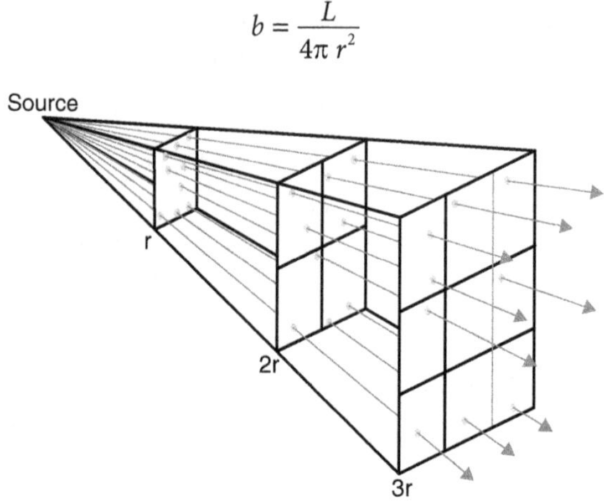

Brightness decreases in proportion to the square of the distance because the area increases with the square of the distance.

PLANETARY SYSTEMS: OUR SOLAR SYSTEM AND OTHERS

Contents of Our Solar System

The Solar System

The **solar system** is our **planetary system**. It consists of the sun and the objects that orbit it: eight planets, two dwarf planets, and numerous asteroids, comets, Kuiper Belt Objects, and gas dust and debris.

The sun itself accounts for ~99.86% of the mass in the solar system. Yet the remaining 0.14% still adds up to $\sim 2.8 \times 10^{24}$ kg of material from which to make everything else in the solar system!

All planets (and most other objects) in the solar system orbit at or very near the **ecliptic plane** in line with the sun's equator. The angular deviance of an orbit from that plane is called an object's **orbital inclination**.

What is a planet?

The definition of a **planet** is an astronomical body orbiting a star or stellar remnant that (1) is massive enough to be rounded by its own gravity, (2) is not massive enough to cause thermonuclear fusion, and (3) has cleared its orbital path.

Requirement 1 means that small, irregularly-shaped objects such as asteroids cannot be planets. Requirement 2 rules out stars, even those that orbit other stars. Requirement 3, added by the International Astronomical Union (IAU) in 2006, means that objects like Pluto and Ceres, which meet the other two requirements, are not planets.

This decision was made in light of the discovery of many objects in the outer solar system that fit the first two requirements. In addition, there appeared to be no reason not to call Ceres a planet under earlier definitions. Instead of changing the order of the planets by adding Ceres, the largest object in the asteroid belt between Mars and Jupiter, while also adding potentially many more outer system objects, the decision was made to classify Ceres and Pluto as **dwarf planets**.

The Terrestrial Planets

The **terrestrial planets** are the inner, rocky worlds of the solar system. These are, in order from the sun, **Mercury**, **Venus**, **Earth**, and **Mars**. These planets are primarily composed of refractory materials like silicate rocks in a crust and mantle surrounding a metallic core, mostly iron and nickel. They have a solid **planetary surface** that has been shaped by comet and asteroid impacts and tectonic forces, though only on earth have plate tectonics been observed. Three of the four terrestrial planets have atmospheres substantial enough to have weather (Venus, Earth, and Mars), while Mercury only has a tenuous atmosphere.

Mercury

The closest planet to the sun (0.4 AU), Mercury is also the smallest planet in the solar system, at 0.055 $M_\oplus$ (1 $M_\oplus$ = 1 earth mass). Mercury has no natural satellites. Its surface is marked by impact craters and wrinkled ridges called **rupes**. Mercury's atmosphere is very tenuous, consisting mostly of atoms scoured from its surface by the solar wind. It does not, as might be thought, have the hottest surface of the planets, as its lack of atmosphere means that it does not retain heat, leading to its night side being cold.

Venus

Venus, the second planet from the sun (0.7 AU), has been called earth's "twin." At 0.815 $M_{\oplus}$, it is the closest in size to the earth. Like the earth, it has evidence of internal geological activity (though not plate tectonics), and a thick atmosphere. However, Venus's atmosphere is about 90 times denser than earth's, consisting of more than 96% carbon dioxide. This means that the surface atmospheric pressure on Venus is about 92 times that of earth, like being 900 m underwater on earth. Carbon dioxide is a **greenhouse gas**, meaning it readily traps heat. Venus's thick atmosphere also has opaque clouds of sulfuric acid droplets. This and Venus's close position to the sun mean that Venus is *very* hot. The mean surface temperature of 735 K (462°C) is hot enough to melt lead. Venus is also very dry. Any surface water it might have had has long since been driven off, leaving the surface a desert.

Venus is the only planet to rotate around its axis clockwise in a **retrograde rotation** (when viewed from the perspective above Earth's North Pole). It also rotates very slowly, completing one rotation every 243 Earth days, shorter than the Venusian year of 224.7 Earth days.

Earth

The earth, our home planet, is the third planet from the sun. It is the largest and densest of the terrestrial planets. It has one natural satellite, the moon, which is the largest satellite with respect to its parent planet in the solar system, at almost $\frac{1}{3}$ the diameter of the earth. The current theory of the moon's formation is the *giant impact hypothesis*, in which a large terrestrial planetesimal, called **Theia**, impacted the early earth. The heavier elements merged with the earth, sinking into its core, while the lighter elements formed a ring which quickly coalesced into the moon.

Earth is the only place where life is known to exist. It is unique in the solar system in having a liquid **hydrosphere**, with free liquid water always present. 71% of earth's surface is covered in liquid water in the form of oceans, lakes, and rivers. This water is thought to be the result of comet impacts in the early solar system.

Earth is the only terrestrial planet with current surface geological activity. Earth's solid inner core of iron and nickel is surrounded by a liquid outer core, a convective mantle and crust of largely silicate minerals. Convection in the mantle drives **plate tectonics** in the earth's **lithosphere**, the upper crust of solid rock. This motion continually recycles crust material down into the mantle, while producing new crust, meaning much of the earth's surface is relatively young compared to the age of the earth.

The motion of the liquid outer core generates earth's strong **magnetic field**, which in turn shields the earth's surface from energetic solar radiation and the particles of the solar wind.

Earth's atmosphere is unique in the solar system for the amount of oxygen, a result of life processes over billions of years. The atmosphere consists of approximately 78% nitrogen, 21% oxygen, ~1% water vapor and argon, with the remaining atmosphere consisting of trace amounts of carbon dioxide, methane, and noble gases such as neon and helium. This atmosphere drives weather, which is an important force in continually shaping the earth's surface through erosion.

The atmosphere is important in protecting life from solar radiation. The **ozone layer** in the upper atmosphere absorbs incoming solar UV radiation that would otherwise be harmful to life on the earth's surface.

Mars

Mars, the fourth planet from the sun (1.5 AU), is smaller than the earth and Venus at 0.107 $M_{\oplus}$. Mars has a carbon dioxide atmosphere at roughly 0.6% Earth's atmospheric pressure. Mars is covered with volcanos, including the largest mountain in the solar system—the vast shield volcano Olympus Mons. The volcanos and other features, such as huge rift valleys, show that Mars was once geologically active; however, there is no current evidence of ongoing geological activity. There is evidence from surface features and minerals that Mars once had surface liquid water, but currently all water on Mars appears to be frozen in its polar ice caps or underground. The surface of Mars is red from large amounts of iron oxide in its soil. Mars has two tiny natural satellites, Phobos and Deimos. They are thought to be asteroids captured from the asteroid belt.

The Asteroid Belt

Between the orbits of Mars and Jupiter (2.2–3.2 AU), separating the terrestrial inner planets of the solar system from the gaseous outer planets, lies the asteroid belt. **Orbital resonances** with Jupiter, where the orbital periods fall into fixed integer ratios, make portions of the asteroid belt region either stable, resulting in clumps of asteroids (the 3:2, 4:3, and 1:1 resonances), or unstable, ejecting masses that fall in those regions (the 4:1, 3:1, 5:2, 7:3, and 2:1 resonances). These orbital resonances make it hard for planet-sized bodies to form gravitationally, and also make the orbits of large bodies in the asteroid belt unstable in the long run. Objects in the asteroid belt range in size from tiny grains to the dwarf planet **Ceres** (2.77 AU, 0.00015 $M_{\oplus}$). The composition of these asteroids falls into three main groups: carbonaceous (C-type), silicate (S-type), and metal-rich (M-type).

The total mass of all objects in the asteroid belt is small, only ~4% of the mass of the moon. More than half the mass of the asteroid belt is contained in the four largest objects: Ceres, Vesta, Pallas, and Hygiea. There are over 200 asteroids known to be over 100 km in diameter, and between 1.1 million and 1.7 million asteroids with a diameter of one km or more. This mass is distributed over a vast area of space, meaning the asteroid belt is very diffuse.

The Giant Planets

Located in the outer solar system, beyond the asteroid belt, are the **giant planets**, also known as the **Jovian planets**, after Jove, another name for the god Jupiter. These planets in order of distance from the sun are **Jupiter**, **Saturn**, **Uranus**, and **Neptune**. These are massive planets composed primarily of volatile materials such as gas and ice, rather than the rocky material of the terrestrial planets. Jupiter and Saturn are sometimes grouped together by composition as the **gas giants**, while Uranus and Neptune are grouped as the **ice giants**. The giant planets are thought to have small solid cores. The composition of these cores is unknown, but is theorized to be molten, with a rocky composition, possibly surrounded by gases compressed by the vast pressure into metallic form.

Jupiter

Jupiter, the fifth planet from the sun (5.2 AU), is 2.5 times the mass of all the other planets put together, at 318 $M_{\oplus}$. It is composed primarily of hydrogen and helium, with an outer atmosphere that is segregated into distinct bands at different latitudes, with turbulence and storms along their boundaries. Prominent among these storms is the **Great Red Spot**. Jupiter has an intense magnetic field, hinting at its internal motion.

Jupiter has 79 known natural satellites, including the four large **Galilean moons: Io**, **Europa**, **Ganymede**, and **Callisto**. Europa is believed to have a liquid water ocean under its outer crust of ice, making it a target for exploration as a possible location for extraterrestrial life. Jupiter also possesses a faint ring. Io is the most volcanic spot in the solar system, with a surface continually reshaped by volcanic activity. This volcanic activity is thought to be due to the intense gravitational forces acting on Io from Jupiter and the other Galilean moons, which knead and heat the interior of Io.

Jupiter has captured many asteroids, both as moons and at its L4 and L5 solar Lagrange points, preceding and following it in its orbit, known as **Trojan asteroids**. They are named after characters from the Iliad, with the preceding group known as the Greek camp, and the following group as the Trojan camp.

Saturn

Saturn, the sixth planet from the sun (9.6 AU), is distinguished by its extensive ring. Saturn has 60% the volume of Jupiter, but is less than a third the mass, at 95 $M_{\oplus}$. Saturn is the least dense planet in the solar system, and is less dense than water. Its composition is much like Jupiter's—primarily hydrogen and helium.

Saturn has 62 known natural satellites (moons), the largest of which are the rocky **Titan** and **Rhea**. Saturn's other moons are mostly ice. Titan is the second-largest moon in the solar system, larger than the planet Mercury, and the only satellite in the solar system with a substantial atmosphere.

Saturn's **planetary rings**, sheets of particles orbiting the planet, are primarily composed of water ice. The rings extend outward 6,630 to 120,700 km from Saturn in distinct bands, but are only on average 20 m thick.

Uranus

Uranus, the seventh planet from the sun (19.2 AU), is also the lightest outer planet at 14.5 $M_{\oplus}$. Uranus, along with Neptune, is an **ice giant**, composed primarily of methane, ammonia, and water ices, with traces of other hydrocarbons, in contrast with the hydrogen and helium of Jupiter and Saturn. Uranus has the solar system's coldest atmosphere, with a minimum temperature of 49 K (–224°C).

Like the other giant planets of the outer solar system, Uranus has a ring system, a magnetosphere, and numerous moons (27 known). Uranus is unique in having an extreme axial tilt, over ninety degrees from the ecliptic. It is theorized that Uranus was struck by a large impactor sometime in the past, causing the unusual tilt.

Neptune

The outermost planet, eighth from the sun (30.1 AU), is Neptune. Though Neptune is slightly smaller than Uranus, the other ice giant, it is more massive ($17\ M_{\oplus}$). It also radiates more internal heat, making its atmosphere warmer than Uranus despite being farther from the sun. Neptune has 14 known satellites, the largest of which, **Triton**, is geologically active, with geysers of liquid nitrogen. Neptune is also accompanied by several minor planets, the **Neptune Trojans**, which maintain a 1:1 orbital resonance.

The Kuiper Belt

Outside the orbit of Neptune, the **trans-Neptunian region**, lies a doughnut-shaped area known as the **Kuiper Belt**. This ring of debris is similar to the asteroid belt, but much larger in volume, extending from ~30 to ~50 AU. **Kuiper Belt objects (KBOs)** are composed mostly of ices of water, methane, and ammonia. They include anything from dozens to thousands of dwarf planets, including **Pluto** (the largest KBO), Makemake, and Haumea, as well as other named objects, including Sedna, Quaoar, Varuna, Orcus, and Eris. The Kuiper Belt itself was once thought to be the source of **short-period comets**, but it is now believed that the **scattered disk**, a region that overlaps the Kuiper Belt and extends much father out, is the true source.

The Oort Cloud

The **Oort cloud** is a theorized region of up to a trillion icy objects surrounding the solar system out to 50,000 AU or even as far as 100,000 AU. It is thought to be the source of all **long-period comets** that visit the solar system. This region remains almost entirely unmapped.

Formation and Evolution of Planetary Systems

The Nebular Hypothesis

- The solar system formed from a collapsing molecular cloud of interstellar gas and dust, a **pre-solar nebula**.
- Conservation of angular momentum caused the pre-solar nebula to rotate faster and flatten into a **protoplanetary disc** of diameter ~200 AU.
- A hot, dense **protostar** formed at the center of the disc.
- Planets formed from gas and dust in the disc, attracting each other via gravitation—a process called **accretion**.

Differentiation

- Due to their higher boiling points, only metals and silicates could exist in the inner solar system near the sun, forming the rocky terrestrial planets and asteroids. There was only a small amount of these materials in the pre-solar nebula, so the terrestrial planets didn't grow as large as the outer planets.
- The outer giant planets formed beyond the **frost line**, where gas and **volatiles** (such as ices) could form. There was more of this material, so the giant planets could grow to be giants.

The Sun Ignites

- After ~50 million years, the pressure and density of hydrogen at the center of the protostar was enough to ignite **thermonuclear fusion**. The temperature, pressure, and density increased until the outward thermal pressure balanced the force of gravity, at which point **hydrostatic equilibrium** was achieved.
- The **solar wind**, the flux of particles from the sun, swept away all the remaining gas and dust from the protoplanetary disk into interstellar space, ending planetary formation.

Exoplanets

- Extra-solar planets, or **exoplanets**, are planets outside of our solar system circling stars other than our sun.
- Exoplanets are hard to detect as they are cool, much smaller than their parent stars, and orbit in ways that are hard to predict from earth observation.
- Exoplanet searches that rely on imaging are usually in the IR spectrum, as they are heated by their star, unlike stars that emit all wavelengths.

Detection Methods

- Direct imaging: Not usually feasible with current instruments
- Transit method: Requires specific geometry to carry the exoplanet between the star and earth
- Microlensing: Also requires specific geometry
- Doppler wobble method: Detects movement in parent star by red/blueshift of the spectrum
- It is harder to detect smaller, farther out planets; therefore, many of the exoplanets we have been able to detect are larger and/or close to their parent stars. **Hot Jupiters** must have formed farther out past the frost point and then migrated closer to their stars.

Habitability and Life in the Universe

- Life is theorized to require liquid water.
- Exoplanets that could have liquid water are said to be in their parent stars' **circumstellar habitable zone** (CHZ) or **"Goldilocks" zone**, since they are "not too hot, not too cold, but just right."

THE SUN AND STARS: NATURE AND EVOLUTION

Our Star, the Sun

The Sun as a Star

Our sun is a typical star. At ~5 billion years old, it is approximately halfway through its projected lifetime.

- The sun's **stellar classification** is as a G2-type main sequence yellow dwarf.
- The sun is composed primarily of hydrogen and helium.
- The sun, like all stars, shines due to thermonuclear fusion.
    - The main fusion pathway in the sun is the **proton–proton chain reaction**: four protons fuse to form one helium nucleus, neutrinos, positrons, and energy equal to the difference in mass (in the form of gamma rays).

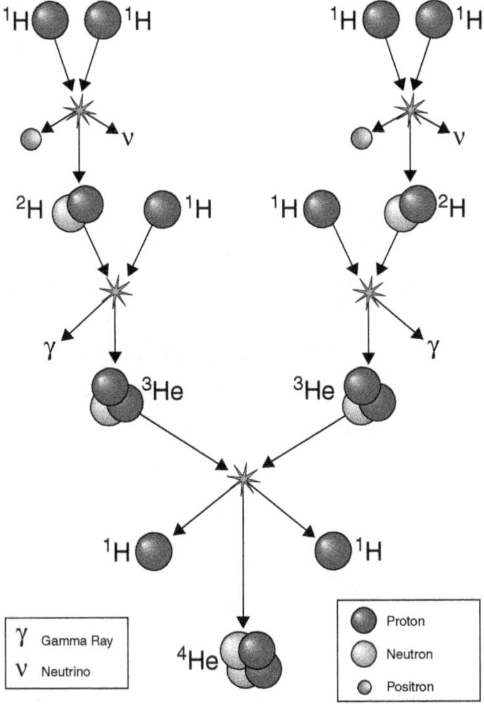

Nuclear fusion in the sun: the proton-proton chain reaction

- Outward pressure due to the temperature of the reaction counteracts the inward pressure of gravity in an effort to achieve **hydrostatic equilibrium**.

Layers of the Sun

The sun, like all stars, is structured in several layers:

- **Core:** The sun's core is where thermonuclear fusion takes place. Temperatures in the core range as high as ~15.7 million K.
- **Radiative zone:** The radiative zone is the portion of the sun from the core to about 0.7 solar radii, where energy is transferred primarily by **thermal radiation**. Photons are emitted, travel a short distance, and are reabsorbed, then re-emitted. Temperatures range from ~2 million K to ~7 million K.
- **Convection zone:** The convection zone extends from 0.7 solar radii to near the sun's surface. It is separated from the radiative zone by the *tachocline*. In this layer, the plasma is not dense enough to transfer heat via thermal radiation, and instead energy transfer occurs via convection, with hot material rising, cooling, and falling back, like a boiling pot. Temperature falls from ~2 million K to ~5,800 K near the surface.

- **Photosphere:** The photosphere is the sun's visible surface, below which the solar plasma becomes opaque to visible light. Photons produced here escape the sun through the solar atmosphere as sunlight.
- **Chromosphere:** Above the photosphere, the temperature drops to a minimum of about 4,100 K at about 500 km above the surface. Above this region, the temperature rapidly increases to ~20,000 K in a region called the chromosphere, so called because light shining through this part of the solar atmosphere produces the **solar emission spectrum**.
- **Corona:** Above the chromosphere is the sun's corona, a region of diffuse particles streaming out from the sun in the solar wind. Though the particle density is only around 10^{-15} to 10^{-16} g/cm^3, for unknown reasons, the average energy of each particle is very high, leading to average temperatures in the corona of 1–2 million K.

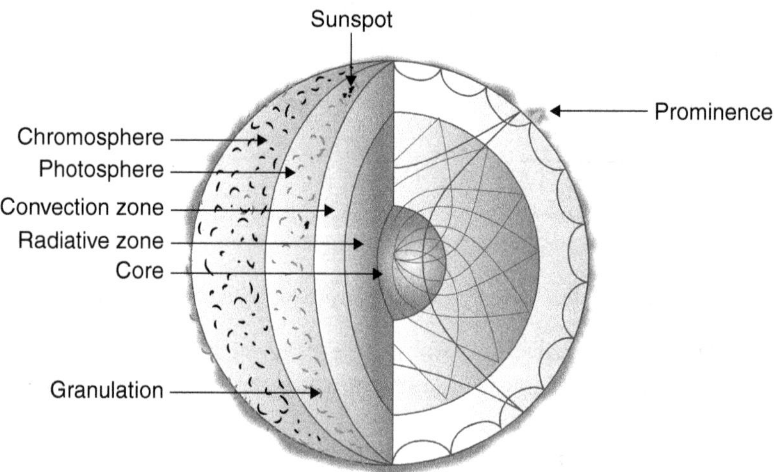

The structure of the sun

Solar Features

- **Sunspots**
  - The sun's photosphere is broken up into cells called granules by the convection from below. Dark areas on the photosphere, called sunspots, are places where magnetic activity inhibits convection, leading to a relatively cooler area of the photosphere.
  - The **sunspot cycle** is the 11-year cycle over which the number of sunspots visible on the sun's photosphere varies from maximum to minimum and back.

- **Solar flares, solar prominences, and coronal mass ejections**
  - The magnetically heated solar atmosphere exhibits a number of different phenomena that release energy in sudden eruptions.
  - **Solar flares** are sudden bright flashes visible in the sun's limb, the edge of the visible solar disk. They are associated with large releases of energy.
  - Flares are sometimes accompanied by **coronal mass ejection (CMEs)**, events where a large burst of energetic particles is released from the sun's corona.
  - **Solar prominences** are large, bright gaseous features that extend thousands of kilometers from the photosphere. These often appear as a loop, where the electrically charged plasma follows along magnetic field lines.
- **The solar wind**
  - Streams of plasma are released from the upper layers of the solar atmosphere and accelerated outward into the solar system by the sun's magnetic field. This stream of charged particles is called the **solar wind**, and consists of mostly protons and electrons. This wind, and the flares and CMEs that periodically occur, causes **space weather**. This "weather" can cause significant **solar storms** that damage space- and ground-based electrical equipment. This is also what causes the **aurora** at the earth's poles.

Properties and Classification of Stars

Stellar Classifications

- Stars are classified based on their emission spectrum, where each line indicates an element or molecule in the star's makeup, and the equivalent width of each line indicates the element's abundance.
- The **spectral class** is assigned to a star based on the star's surface temperature. The system in most common use is the **Morgan–Keenan system**, which uses the letters O, B, A, F, G, K, and M from hottest to coolest. Each letter class is further divided into numbers from 0 (the hottest) to 9 (the coolest).
- Plotting the temperature/spectral class of stars versus their luminosity/apparent magnitude produces the **Hertzsprung–Russell diagram (H–R diagram)**.
- Natural groupings appear when stars are plotted on the Hertzsprung–Russell diagram. These are **luminosity classes**, and correspond to the size and brightness of the stars in each group. The majority of stars fall into a path called the **main sequence**.
- A Roman numeral is added to the spectral class of a star to denote its luminosity class:

- Class 0 or Ia+: hypergiants
- Class I: supergiants
- Class II: bright giants
- Class III: giants
- Class IV: sub-giants
- Class V: dwarfs or main-sequence stars
- Class sd or VI: sub-dwarfs
- Class D or VII: white dwarfs

- Our sun is classified as a G2V star: It is a main-sequence star with a surface temperature of around 5,700 K, a so-called yellow dwarf.

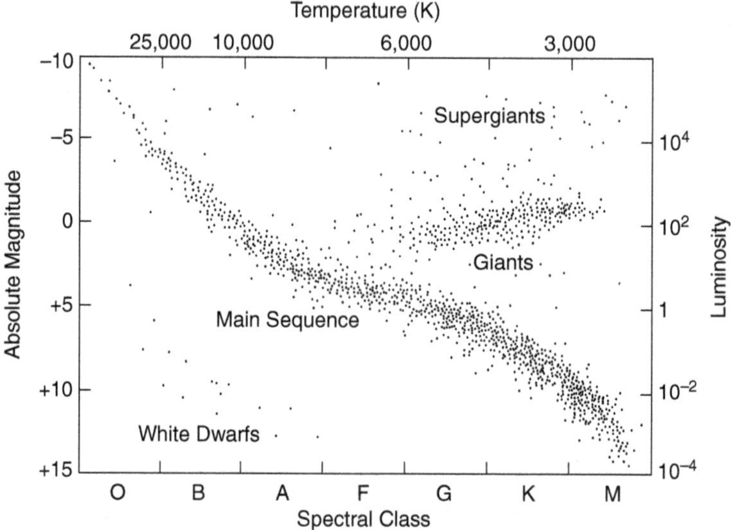

The Hertzsprung–Russell diagram

Birth, Life, and Death of Stars

Star Birth

- As discussed when talking about the birth of the solar system, stars are formed from the gravitational collapse of a molecular cloud of gas and dust into a **stellar nebula**, which forms into a disk, due to conservation of angular momentum.
- A **protostar** forms at the center of this spinning disk, as gas and dust is concentrated further due to gravity.

- While the protostar is hot due to the pressure of the in-falling gas, it isn't a true star until the pressure is high enough in the core to initiate **thermonuclear fusion**.
- Radiation from the thermonuclear reaction counteracts the collapse due to gravity, and **hydrostatic equilibrium** is reached.
- Objects that are not quite large enough to start fusing hydrogen—but are still larger and hotter than planets—are called **brown dwarfs**.
- Stars often form in groupings from the same clouds of gas, called **stellar nurseries**. The radiation from the new stars eventually causes the remaining gas and dust to disperse, halting stellar formation.

Star Life

- Larger stars are more luminous, as they fuse more of their fuel at a given time than smaller, less luminous stars. However, this means that larger, more luminous stars also have shorter lifetimes than smaller stars, as their fuel runs out more quickly.
- As they go through their lives, stars follow an evolutionary path through the Hertzsprung–Russell diagram, changing spectral class and luminosity.
    - A star like the sun starts its life on the main-sequence path.
    - As hydrogen fuel runs out in the core of the star, fusion ceases there, leaving a core of helium, which shrinks and heats. This then drives **hydrogen-shell burning** in the layers around the helium core. The star actually gets brighter, and moves away from the main sequence to the **sub-giant branch**.
    - The increased luminosity causes the outer layers to expand greatly, and the star becomes a **red giant**.
    - As more and more helium falls into the core of the star, the increased pressure causes helium to fuse into carbon in the **triple-alpha process:**

$$^{4}\text{He} + {}^{4}\text{He} \rightarrow {}^{8}\text{Be} + \text{energy}$$
$$^{8}\text{Be} + {}^{4}\text{He} \rightarrow {}^{12}\text{C} + \text{energy}$$

    - The increase of energy and core temperature does not change the pressure, due to **electron degeneracy** supporting the core instead of outward thermal pressure. Eventually, thermal pressure takes over, leading to a sudden **helium flash**.
    - The star's core is now stable and fusing hydrogen, but it is less luminous because the helium flash has expanded and cooled the core. The star enters the **horizontal branch** of the H–R diagram.

- As helium-burning slows, the star again expands and reenters the giant group on the **asymptotic giant branch**, now with a core of carbon.
- Lacking the mass to fuse carbon, a sun-like star ceases most fusion in its core and cools. The outer layers continue to fuse and expand, cooling and heating in pulses, until the outer layers are ejected entirely, forming a **planetary nebula**.

Star Death

When a star reaches the end of its life, its fate will depend upon its mass. What remains is called a **stellar remnant**.

- **White dwarfs:**
  - A star like the sun ejects its outer layers as a planetary nebula. What remains is a **white dwarf**, a small, dense, cooling carbon core. This will be the fate of the sun at the end of its approximately 10-billion-year lifetime, 5 billion years from now.
- **Supernovae and neutron stars:**
  - For larger stars, fusion does not stop at carbon. Heavier elements can continue to fuse in progressive shells around the core. As each element is consumed, the core contracts, heats up, and fuses the next element in the chain. This continues until iron is produced. Fusion of iron atoms into lead would be a net energy loss.
  - Without outward thermal pressure, the core contracts and heats to ~10 billion K. This breaks all the atoms in the core into elementary particles (protons, neutrons, and electrons) via **photodisintigration**. This cools the core, causing it to collapse even faster.
  - Electrons are crushed together with protons to form neutrons and neutrinos: $p + e \rightarrow n + \nu$
  - The core now abruptly collapses until the neutrons are in direct contact. This stops the collapse suddenly, and the collapsing gas rebounds from the solid neutron core, exploding the outer layers of the star in a supernova.
  - The released energy not only blows the outer layers of the star outward into a nebula but also supplies enough energy to cause the fusion of elements beyond iron, a process called **stellar nucleosynthesis**. This is the source of all elements heavier than iron in the universe, seeding future generations of stars and planets.

    - In addition to the nebula, the core of neutrons is left behind as a dense, hot mass called a **neutron star**.
    - These stellar remnants have intense magnetic fields and are often powerful radiation sources in the gamma and X-ray ranges. Spinning neutron stars whose beams of radiation periodically sweeps across the earth are called **pulsars**.
- **Black holes**
    - For even more massive stars—those above the **Chandrasekhar limit**—not even the **neutron degeneracy pressure** (pressure caused by neutrons trying to escape their quantum states) is enough to stop the core collapse.
    - The smallest size reached is unknown. According to general relativity it could be an infinitely dense **singularity**.
    - The resultant object is called a **black hole** because the density is so high that even light is bent on paths that can't escape the singularity.

GALAXIES

Our Galaxy, the Milky Way

Milky Way Classification and Characteristics

- Our galaxy, the Milky Way, is a **barred spiral galaxy**.
- It is ~100,000 light years (30 kiloparsecs) in diameter and approximately 1,000 ly (0.3 kpc) thick.
- The mass of the Milky Way is approximately 1.5 trillion solar masses. Most of this mass is dark matter.
- The Milky Way contains between 200 and 400 billion stars.

Structure of the Milky Way

Seen edge-on, the Milky Way has a distinct large-scale structure: The circular **galactic disk**, where our solar system lies, swells into a **galactic bulge** at the center. The disk and bulge are embedded in a roughly spherical ball of older stars called the **galactic halo**.

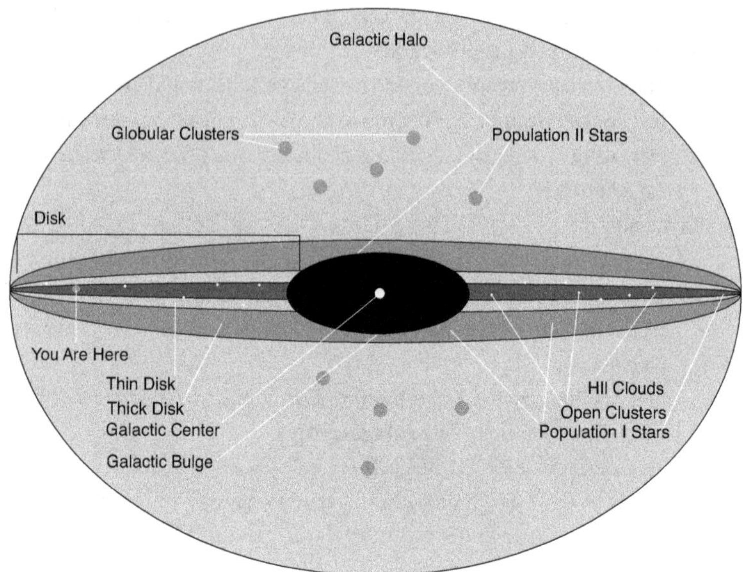

The structure of the Milky Way

- **The galactic disk**
  - The galactic disk is a circular, flattened region broken up into the relatively bright areas of the **spiral arms** and alternating with darker (in visible and UV light) areas.
  - The spiral arms of the Milky Way and galaxies like it are brighter because that is where most of the new star formation takes place, so newer, more luminous stars are more abundant there.
  - The spiral arms of the Milky Way cannot rotate along with the Galaxy, as they would curl up. They must be density waves. This accounts for the star formation, as gas is relatively more dense there, forming molecular clouds that become stellar nurseries.

- **The galactic bulge and the galactic center**
  - The galactic disk swells in the center to a fatter bulge.
  - Our view of the center of the Milky Way is blocked by gas and dust that is opaque to visible light. It can be imaged in the X-ray and infrared ranges of the EM spectrum, which can pass through the intervening clouds.
  - The galactic center contains hundreds of thousands of closely-packed stars around a strong radio source, **Sagittarius A***, which is now known to be a supermassive black hole, 4.1–4.5 million times the mass of the sun.

- **The galactic halo**
  - Surrounding the galactic disk and bulge are the old stars comprising the galactic halo. All the stars are older because no active star formation takes place in the halo.
  - Many of these old stars are tightly packed into **globular clusters** orbiting the galactic center. Stars in these clusters are tightly bound by gravity, unlike **open clusters** of stars in the galactic disk.

The Rotation Curve of the Milky Way and the Case for Dark Matter

- Orbital velocities of objects (stars, luminous nebula, etc.) in the galaxy can be determined from the redshift of known emission lines, like the 21-cm emission of neutral hydrogen.
- Plotting the orbital velocities of visible objects versus their distance from the galactic center produces a **rotation curve**.
- If the brightest parts of the galaxy have the most mass, trailing off into the disk, then we can use Kepler's laws to predict that the rotation curve of the Milky Way (and other spiral galaxies) would be high near the center of the galaxy and trail off to slower orbital velocities farther out.
- The actual rotation curve of observed spiral galaxies shows that they are **flat rotation curves** that extend to well outside the visible disk. Therefore, matter in the galaxy is not distributed in a way that matches their visible light output. Some sort of **dark matter**, as much as 95% of the total galactic mass, exists throughout the galaxy and extends in a **dark matter halo** far beyond the visible extent of the galactic disk.

Galactic Neighborhood

- The Milky Way has several small companion galaxies, the two largest of which are the **Small** and **Large Magellanic Clouds**.
- The **Andromeda galaxy**, our nearest neighbor galaxy, is a spiral galaxy ~780 kpc from the Milky Way. It is thought to be approximately the same mass as the Milky Way, but is wider—about 220,000 ly in diameter. It is expected to collide with the Milky Way in approximately 4.5 billion years.
- The Milky Way and the Andromeda galaxy are part of the **Local Group**, a group of 50 closely bound galaxies.

Classification and Structure of Galaxies

Galactic Classification

Galaxies are classified according to their shape. This classification is sometimes arranged in a **Hubble tuning fork diagram**, invented by astronomer Edwin Hubble in 1926.

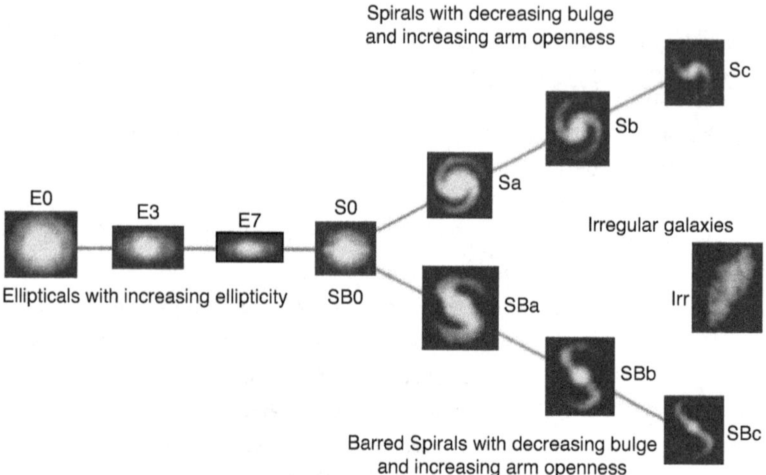

The Hubble tuning fork diagram of galactic classification

- **Elliptical galaxies** lie at one end of the diagram. They are smooth, featureless light distributions, and are classified from near-circular (**E0**) to mostly flattened (**E7**).
- **Lenticular galaxies**, classified as **S0**, lie at the point where the diagram branches. They have a bright central bulge, surrounded by a disk structure with no arms visible.
- The **spiral galaxies** form two parallel branches on the diagram. Spiral galaxies have a flattened disk and central bulge, with the disk arranged in a spiral structure.
    - Half of all spiral galaxies have a bar-like structure extending from the central bulge which then branches into the spiral arms. These are called **barred spiral galaxies**.
    - The other spiral galaxies do not have this bar structure, and are called regular spiral galaxies, or simply **spiral galaxies**.
    - Spirals are classified with the letter **S**, while barred spirals use **SB**. They range from **Sa (SBa)** for tightly wound spirals to **Sd (SBd)** for very loose spirals.

- Irregular galaxies do not fit in the Hubble tuning fork diagram because they lack a definable structure or are asymmetric. They are classified as **Irr**.

Active Galaxies and Active Galactic Nuclei (AGN)

- The luminosity of most **normal galaxies** ranges from ~10^6 solar luminosities (dwarf galaxies) to ~10^{12} solar luminosities for very large elliptical galaxies.
- As many as 40% of bright galaxies (above 10^{10} solar luminosities) have a luminosity much larger than their size would normally explain and emit radiation in significantly different parts of the EM spectrum than normal galaxies. These are called **active galaxies.**
- There are many different types of active galaxies. The source of their emissions is usually in or near their cores, called **active galactic nuclei** (**AGN**).
    - **Seyfert galaxies:**
        - Normal spiral galaxies whose nucleus is ~10,000 times brighter than the center of the Milky Way
        - Emit radiation in a broad spectrum, but centered on the IR
        - Emissions often vary over time, creating pulses
        - Thought to be caused by violent non-stellar activity in the core of the galaxy, like matter falling into their central black hole
    - **Radio galaxies:**
        - Active in the radio portion to the EM spectrum
        - Energy released not from the nucleus, but from huge extended regions called **radio lobes**, about ten times the size of the Milky Way
        - Caused by material thought to be ejected at high velocity from the galactic nuclei
    - **Quasars:**
        - Short for **quasi-stellar radio sources**
        - Due to material falling into a supermassive black hole of millions or billions of solar masses
        - Very luminous (10 to 10,000 times the luminosity of the Milky Way), but very distant (between 600 million and 29 billion light years away from the earth) and receding at a very high redshift, meaning that they were more common in the early universe

Measuring Cosmic Distances

- **Stellar parallax** can be used to measure relatively close objects, like nearby stars, but it is impractical for larger distances.
- The apparent brightness of objects of known luminosity, called **standard candles**, are measured to construct a **distance ladder**.

- **Variable stars**, which vary in luminosity over a fixed period, are used as standard candles.
    - **RR Lyrae variables** are low-mass stars on the horizontal branch of the Hertzsprung–Russell diagram that have evolved off the main sequence and are unstable, pulsing their luminosity as the core cools and shrinks. They all have approximately the same luminosity, which can be immediately known once they are recognized.
    - **Cepheid variables** are high-mass stars in the unstable portion of the horizontal branch of the H–R diagram. Their pulsation can be directly correlated to their luminosity, known as the **period–luminosity relationship**.
- For longer distances, **Type I supernovae** are used as standard candles. All of this type of supernovae are known to have nearly the same luminosity.
- Active galactic nuclei can extend the distance ladder even farther, though the values for their luminosities are less well known.

THE UNIVERSE: CONTENTS, STRUCTURE, AND EVOLUTION

Galaxy Clusters and Large-Scale Structure

- The **Local Group** is a bound group of about 50 galaxies, including the Milky Way and the Andromeda galaxies, surrounded by the **Local Void**. It has a diameter of ~3 megaparsecs (Mpc).
- The Local Group is, in turn, part of the **Virgo Supercluster** of galaxies, consisting of at least 100 galaxy groups and clusters in a 33-Mpc diameter space.
- The Virgo Supercluster is part of an even larger supercluster, the **Laniakea Supercluster**, which is centered on a gravitational anomaly called the **Great Attractor**.
- The largest-scale structures in the universe are **galactic filaments**, **galactic walls**, and **galactic sheets**. These form a foam-like structure around vast empty spaces called **cosmic voids**.

The Big Bang and Hubble's Law

- In the 1920s, Edwin Hubble and colleagues discovered that the emission and absorption spectra of galaxies they were observing was always redshifted, meaning they were moving away from us, and that more distant galaxies were more redshifted:

- **Hubble's law:** *The velocity at which a galaxy is moving away from us is proportional to the distance to that galaxy*, or

$$v_r = H_0 \times d_G,$$

  where v_r is the **recessional velocity**, d_G is the distance to the galaxy, and H_0 is the **Hubble constant**.
- Hubble's law would be true no matter where we are in the universe, because space is expanding, carrying everything away from everything else, like points marked on a balloon as it is blown up. The Hubble constant is the rate of that expansion.
- This implies that the universe expanded *from* something, and that, rather than existing in a steady state forever and continuing forever, the universe had a starting point: the **big bang**.

The Evolution and Fate of the Universe

The Universe from the Big Bang to the Present

- **The big bang:** An infinitely dense **singularity** exploded, releasing all the energy in the universe. This event was the big bang.
- **Inflation:** For a brief time after the big bang (10^{-35} to 10^{-33} seconds), the new universe expanded much faster than the speed of light, and, for reasons not yet totally understood, increasing more than 1,030 times in size—a process called **inflation**. This explains two problems.
  - **The flatness problem:** The universe is too flat.
  - **The uniformity problem:** The cosmic microwave background radiation (see below) is too smooth.
- **Cooling:** The expanding universe cooled until particles could form.
  - **Electron–positron annihilation** left some electrons behind, leading to the existence of matter instead of antimatter in the modern universe.
  - **Nucleosynthesis:** Protons and neutrons formed the first atomic nuclei, predominantly hydrogen, with some helium.
  - **Cosmic Microwave Background:** Around 377,000 years after the big bang, the universe cools enough for electrons to be captured by nuclei, meaning that photons could now travel long distances without immediately being reabsorbed and re-emitted. At this point, the universe is transparent to radiation. This **surface of last scattering** is the earliest visible part of the universe, and the radiation from this surface, now redshifted to the microwave portion of the EM spectrum, forms the **cosmic microwave background (CMB) radiation**.

        - Measurements of the CMB can be used to pinpoint the age of the universe at 13.8 billion years.
    - **Structure formation:** Formation of the first stars and galaxies took place about 150 million to 1 billion years after the big bang.
    - **Accelerating expansion:** Beginning about 9.8 billion years after the big bang, the expansion of the universe stopped decelerating due to gravity and began to accelerate. This **accelerating expansion of the universe** does not have a precise known cause. Some unknown form of dark energy is counteracting the gravity of the normal mass/energy of the universe, causing it to expand at an increasing pace.

Fate of the Universe

- **Accelerating expansion and critical density of the universe:**
    - The fate of the universe depends on its average mass/energy density in relation to the **critical density** required to slow, stop, and reverse the accelerating expansion of the universe.
        - Density parameter, $\Omega_{mass} \frac{\text{actual density of the universe}}{\text{critical density of the universe}}$
        - Ω_{Λ} is the density parameter for dark energy causing accelerating expansion where Λ is the cosmological constant.
- **Spatial curvature:** There are three possible shapes for the space-time of our universe:
    - **Flat universe,** $\Omega_{mass} + \Omega_{\Lambda} = 1$: space is infinite and has a flat geometry.
    - **Open universe,** $\Omega_{mass} + \Omega_{\Lambda} < 1$: space is infinite and has a curved geometry.
    - **Closed universe,** $\Omega_{mass} + \Omega_{\Lambda} > 1$: space is finite and closes back on itself with a curved geometry.
- The three possible fates of the universe:
    - **Big rip:** $\Omega_{mass} < 1$ and gravity is too weak to stop the expansion of the universe, causing it to expand at an increasing rate forever, leading to a "big rip."
    - **Big crunch:** $\Omega_{mass} > 1$ and gravity stops the accelerating expansion of the universe, causing it to collapse into a "big crunch."
    - **Heat death of the universe:** $\Omega_{mass} = 1$ and expansion slows, but never stops. Eventually all matter and energy in the universe is distributed evenly over an infinite space, leading to the "heat death of the universe."
    - Current observations show that the universe is very flat, meaning that **neither a big crunch nor a big rip seem likely to happen**.

Dark Matter and Dark Energy

Dark Matter

- Current best measurements indicate that the energy and mass in the present day universe is divided into:
    - 68% dark energy
    - 27% dark matter
    - 5% normal matter
- The rotational curves of observed galaxies require that more matter be present than is observable as luminous "normal" matter.
- This **dark matter** is not simply normal matter that is not emitting radiation. It must be some sort of unknown form of matter that exhibits the following properties:
    - Does not interact with electromagnetic radiation (and thus is invisible)
    - Only very weakly interacts with normal matter
- Observational evidence of dark matter beyond the rotation curves of galaxies includes the following:
    - **Gravitational lensing** by non-visible mass in observations of background galaxies
    - The **Bullet Cluster**, a collision between two galaxies, where the observed center of mass is far removed from the center of the visible normal mass

Dark Energy

- Dark energy is the unknown form of energy that is hypothesized to permeate all of space, accelerating the expansion of the universe.
- Other than the observation that *something* is causing the expansion to accelerate, little is known about the underlying cause of the acceleration.
- The effects of dark energy might be constant (the **cosmological constant**), or might vary over time and space. Any variation might be very subtle or very slow, and thus difficult to observe.
- Research is ongoing.

SUMMING IT UP

- **Astronomy** is the natural science that studies celestial objects and phenomena. *Observational astronomy* observes celestial objects and phenomena with a wide variety of instruments and techniques, while *theoretical astronomy* applies physics, mathematics, and chemistry to explain observational data and construct theoretical models of the universe.
- The **scientific method** is an approach to investigation of the world around us that involves both thinking and doing. Phenomena are carefully observed, explained via theories, and those theories are tested via experiment, producing more observations, which in turn can be used to predict more phenomena.
- A scientific theory must be (1) testable, (2) tested, and (3) simple. According to **Occam's razor**, the simplest scientific theory to explain all the available observational data is likely the correct one. Adding more variables than necessary to fit data leads to *overfitting*, which in turn leads to poor predictive power in a model.
- The **Ptolemaic model** places the earth, a perfect sphere, at the center of the universe. The sun, moon, and planets move around the earth on **celestial spheres**. Despite containing ideas which have since been disproven, Ptolemy's model was able to accurately predict the motion of planets, and even accounted for the **retrograde motion** observed in some planets, where they seemed to slow down, stop, or even move in reverse.
- The Copernican **heliocentric model** provided a practical alternative to the Ptolemaic model, proposing the following: (1) Heavenly motions are uniform, eternal, and circular or compounded of several circles (epicycles); (2) the center of the universe is near the sun; (3) around the sun, in order, are Mercury, Venus, the earth and moon, Mars, Jupiter, Saturn, and the fixed stars; (4) the earth has three motions: daily rotation, annual revolution, and annual tilting of its axis; and (5) retrograde motion of the planets is explained by the earth's motion.
- **Tycho Brahe** (1546–1601) challenged the heliocentric model by proving that novae were not objects below the orbit of the moon, thus showing that the heavens were not unchanging. He also proved that comets were not atmospheric phenomena, as had been thought, but were objects that must pass through the celestial spheres. Both observations cast further doubt on the Aristotelian beliefs in an unchanging celestial realm.
- **Johannes Kepler** (1571–1630) formulated his **laws of planetary motion** in the early 1600s. One of his theories was that the planets had elliptical orbits, rather than circular.

- The laws discovered by Johannes Kepler are key to the understanding of astrophysics, and include **Kepler's first law:** The orbits of the planets are ellipses with the sun at one focus; **Kepler's second law (the law of areas):** A line from a planet to the sun sweeps over equal areas in equal intervals of time; and **Kepler's third law (the harmonic law):** The square of a planet's orbital period is proportional to the cube of the semi-major axis of its orbit.
- Also in the early 1600s, **Galileo Galilei** made several important discoveries. He found that the moon was in fact covered in mountains and craters. Secondly, Galileo observed that the Milky Way was made up of many stars, with many too faint to see with the naked eye. Thirdly, he observed that Jupiter was circled by what we now call the *Galilean moons*. His discoveries provided strong evidence for the Copernican model by explaining circumstances that the Ptolemaic model could not.
- An **astronomical unit (AU)** is defined as earth's average distance from the sun, defined as one AU = 149,597,870,700 m. A rough value of 150 million km (~93 million miles) can be used for most calculations.
- **Newton's laws of motion**, as well as his **law of universal gravitation**, are fundamental to the study of astrophysics. **Newton's first law (law of inertia)** states that, in an inertial frame of reference, an object either remains at rest or continues to move at a constant velocity unless acted upon by a force.
- **Newton's second law** states that, in an inertial frame of reference, the sum of all forces on an object equals the mass of the object times the acceleration of the object.
- **Newton's third law** states that when one body exerts a force on a second body, the second body simultaneously exerts a force equal in magnitude and opposite in direction on the first body.
- **Newton's law of universal gravitation** states that every point mass in the universe attracts every other point mass with a force that is directly proportional to the product of their masses, and inversely proportional to the square of the distance between them.
- Another concept in physics that is important in astronomy is that of **conserved quantities**—quantities whose values remain constant in a system over time. Many physical laws express some sort of conservation, including **conservation of energy**, **conservation of momentum**, and **conservation of angular momentum**.
- Einstein's first postulate for the **principle of special relativity** states that the laws of physics are the same for all observers in uniform motion relative to one another. Einstein's second postulate for the principle of special relativity deals with the speed of light, and states that the **speed of light in a vacuum is**

constant, with the same value for all observers independent of their motion relative to the light source. The postulates of special relativity have several important consequences, including the ideas that time moves differently under specific situations, and that **the speed of light is a universal limit**.

- Einstein developed his **theory of general relativity** in order to incorporate gravity into his theories of special relativity. This led to the equivalence principle, which states that observers cannot distinguish between inertial forces due to acceleration or uniform gravitational forces due to the presence of a massive body.
- According to the theory of general relativity, mass tells space-time how to curve, and the curvature of space-time tells mass how to accelerate. Thus, in general relativity, gravitational acceleration is not an instantaneous force between objects, but a natural consequence of the *curvature of space-time caused by the presence of mass.*
- The position of celestial objects can be located on the **celestial sphere** using the **celestial coordinate system**. This is analogous to the coordinate system of latitude and longitude used on the earth's surface, but projected onto the inside surface of a sphere.
- As the earth moves though its orbit, the position of the earth changes with respect to stars, a phenomenon known as **parallax**. The earth is on opposite sides of the sun every six months, so observing a star at this interval gives the largest parallax angle, the **annual parallax**. The **parsec (pc)** is a unit defined as the distance of an object for which the annual parallax is one arcsecond, and corresponds to 3.26 light years.
- The moon completes its eastward orbit around the earth in 27.3 days, an interval known as the moon's **sidereal period**. The moon is in a **synchronous orbit** around the earth, meaning its period of rotation is nearly equal to its sidereal period. This means that it keeps one face toward the earth at all times—the **near side of the moon**—and one side pointed permanently away from the earth—**the dark side of the moon**.
- As the moon orbits around the earth, the half of the moon that faces the sun will be lit. A changing portion of that lit face will be visible from earth, known as the **phases of the moon**. These are divided into **eight major phases**: new moon, waxing crescent moon, first quarter moon, waxing gibbous moon, full moon, waning gibbous moon, last quarter moon, and waning crescent moon.
- The cycle of the moon's phases repeats every 29.5 days, known as the moon's **synodic period**.
- A **solar eclipse** occurs when the moon passes between the earth and the sun, blocking the sun's light hitting the earth. This occurs during a new moon, as

the lit side of the moon is facing away from the earth. A **lunar eclipse** occurs when the earth blocks the sun's light from hitting the moon. This can occur during a full moon, as the lit side of the moon is facing the earth at this point.

- Electromagnetic waves can be arranged in an **electromagnetic (EM) spectrum** from high-energy/high-frequency/short-wavelength EM radiation, such as gamma and X-rays, through longer wavelengths such as ultraviolet, visible, and infrared light, to low-energy/low-frequency/long-wavelength EM radiation like microwaves and radio waves.
- The **Doppler effect** is the change in frequency or wavelength of a wave in relation to an observer who is moving relative to the wave source. An everyday example of this effect is the sound a car makes as it approaches you, the pitch of the car noise rising until it passes, and the pitch dropping as it pulls away from you.
- When an object emitting waves moves closer to an observer, the observed waves will decrease in wavelength as each successive wave crest arrives earlier than the one before it. This corresponds to an increase in frequency as more wave peaks arrive at the observer in a given period. This will mean the object's radiation will shift toward the blue end of the spectrum, a phenomenon called **blueshift**. If the object is moving away, the radiation it emits will conversely experience **redshift**.
- **Optical telescopes** come in two basic types: refracting telescopes and reflecting telescopes. A **refracting telescope** uses a lens to gather and concentrate incoming light. The light is refracted (bent) by the **objective lens** to pass through a **focus**, and then gathered and made parallel again by a **secondary lens** or eyepiece to form an image on the detector (or eye). A **reflecting telescope**, on the other hand, uses a primary mirror placed at the bottom of a tube and a flat secondary mirror placed above the tube at the focus to direct the light to the objective lens and detector.
- The continuous spectrum of radiation from a heated object is known as **blackbody radiation**. A **blackbody** is a theoretical object that is a perfect absorber and emitter of radiation. Such an object would appear black at room temperature, thus its name, but would glow at shorter and shorter wavelengths as it was heated.
- The **solar system** is our **planetary system**. It consists of the sun and the objects that orbit it: eight planets, two dwarf planets, numerous asteroids, comets, Kuiper Belt objects, as well as gas, dust, and debris.
- The definition of a **planet** is an astronomical body orbiting a star or stellar remnant that (1) is massive enough to be rounded by its own gravity, (2) is not massive enough to cause thermonuclear fusion, and (3) has cleared its orbital path.

- The **Oort cloud** is a theorized region of up to a trillion icy objects surrounding the solar system out to 50,000 AU or even as far as 100,000 AU. It is thought to be the source of all **long-period comets** that visit the solar system. This region remains almost entirely unmapped.
- One generally accepted theory regarding the beginning and development of the solar system (and galaxies in general) is the **Nebular Hypothesis**, which theorizes that the solar system formed from a collapsing molecular cloud of interstellar gas and dust called a **pre-solar nebula**. Conservation of angular momentum caused the pre-solar nebula to rotate faster and flatten into a **protoplanetary disc** of diameter ~200 AU. A hot, dense **protostar** formed at the center of the disc, and eventually planets formed from gas and dust in the disc, attracting each other via gravitation—a process called **accretion**.
- Exoplanets that could have liquid water are said to be in their parent stars' **circumstellar habitable zone (CHZ)** or **"Goldilocks" zone**, since they are "not too hot, not too cold, but just right."
- The **layers of the sun** include the core, the radiative zone, the convection zone, the photosphere, the chromosphere, and the corona.
- Stars are classified based on their **emission spectrum**, where each line indicates an element or molecule in the star's makeup, and the equivalent width of each line indicates the element's abundance. The **spectral class** is assigned to a star based on the star's surface temperature. The system in most common use is the **Morgan–Keenan system**, which uses the letters **O, B, A, F, G, K,** and **M,** from hottest to coolest. Each letter class is further divided into numbers from 0 (the hottest) to 9 (the coolest).
- Larger stars are more luminous, as they fuse more of their fuel at a given time than smaller, less luminous stars. However, this means that *larger, more luminous stars have shorter lifetimes than smaller stars*, as their fuel runs out more quickly. As they go through their lives, stars follow an evolutionary path through the **Hertzsprung–Russell diagram**, changing spectral class and luminosity.
- When a star reaches the end of its life, its fate will depend upon its mass. What remains is called a **stellar remnant**, which can result in a **white dwarf** or, if the star's remaining mass is sufficient, it may become a **supernova** or a **neutron star**. Stars that are even more massive may become **black holes**.
- Our galaxy is the **Milky Way galaxy**, which has several small companion galaxies, the two largest of which are the **Small** and **Large Magellanic Clouds**. The **Andromeda galaxy**, our nearest neighbor galaxy, is a spiral galaxy ~780 kpc from the Milky Way. The Milky Way and the Andromeda galaxies are part of the **Local Group**, a group of 50 closely bound galaxies.

- Types of galaxies include **elliptical galaxies, lenticular galaxies**, and **spiral galaxies**. Spiral galaxies have a flattened disk and central bulge, with the disk arranged in a spiral structure. Half of all spiral galaxies have a bar-like structure extending from the central bulge which then branches into the spiral arms. These are called **barred spiral galaxies**.
- **Stellar parallax** can be used to measure relatively close objects, like nearby stars, but it is impractical for larger distances.
- The **Local Group** is a bound group of about 50 galaxies including the Milky Way and the Andromeda galaxy, surrounded by the **Local Void**. It has a diameter of ~3 megaparsecs (Mpc). The Local Group is, in turn, part of the **Virgo Supercluster** of galaxies, which is part of an even larger supercluster, the **Laniakea Supercluster**, which is centered on a gravitational anomaly called the **Great Attractor**.
- In the 1920s, Edwin Hubble and colleagues developed **Hubble's law**, which states that galaxies move away from us at a velocity proportionate to their distance. Hubble's law would be true no matter where we are in the universe, because space is expanding, carrying everything away from everything else, like points marked on a balloon as it is blown up. The **Hubble constant** is the rate of that expansion. This implies that the universe expanded *from* something, and that, rather than existing in a steady state forever and continuing forever, the universe had a starting point: the **big bang**.
- The evolution of the universe started with the big bang, in which an infinitely dense singularity exploded, releasing all the energy in the universe. For a fraction of a second after the big bang, the new universe expanded much faster than the speed of light and increased more than 1030 times in size—a process called **inflation**. This was followed by a period during which the universe cooled until particles could form.
- Beginning about 9.8 billion years after the big bang, the expansion of the universe stopped decelerating due to gravity and began to accelerate. This **accelerating expansion of the universe** does not have a precise known cause.
- The fate of the universe depends on what its average mass/energy density is in relation to a **critical density** needed to slow, stop, and reverse the accelerating expansion of the universe. The three possible fates of the universe are the **big rip**, the **big crunch**, and the **heat death of the universe**. Current observations show that the universe is very flat, meaning that neither a big crunch nor a big rip seem likely to happen.
- Current best measurements indicate that the energy and mass in the universe is divided into 68% dark energy, 27% dark matter, and 5% normal matter. The rotational curves of observed galaxies require that more matter be present than is observable as luminous "normal" matter. This **dark matter** is not

simply normal matter that is not emitting radiation. It must be some sort of unknown form of matter that (1) does not interact with electromagnetic radiation (and thus is invisible), and (2) interacts with normal matter very weakly.

- **Dark energy** is the unknown form of energy that is hypothesized to permeate all of space, accelerating the expansion of the universe. Other than the observation that *something* is causing the expansion to accelerate, little is known about the underlying cause of the acceleration.

Chapter 4

Astronomy Post-Test

POST-TEST ANSWER SHEET

1. Ⓐ Ⓑ Ⓒ Ⓓ	18. Ⓐ Ⓑ Ⓒ Ⓓ	35. Ⓐ Ⓑ Ⓒ Ⓓ
2. Ⓐ Ⓑ Ⓒ Ⓓ	19. Ⓐ Ⓑ Ⓒ Ⓓ	36. Ⓐ Ⓑ Ⓒ Ⓓ
3. Ⓐ Ⓑ Ⓒ Ⓓ	20. Ⓐ Ⓑ Ⓒ Ⓓ	37. Ⓐ Ⓑ Ⓒ Ⓓ
4. Ⓐ Ⓑ Ⓒ Ⓓ	21. Ⓐ Ⓑ Ⓒ Ⓓ	38. Ⓐ Ⓑ Ⓒ Ⓓ
5. Ⓐ Ⓑ Ⓒ Ⓓ	22. Ⓐ Ⓑ Ⓒ Ⓓ	39. Ⓐ Ⓑ Ⓒ Ⓓ
6. Ⓐ Ⓑ Ⓒ Ⓓ	23. Ⓐ Ⓑ Ⓒ Ⓓ	40. Ⓐ Ⓑ Ⓒ Ⓓ
7. Ⓐ Ⓑ Ⓒ Ⓓ	24. Ⓐ Ⓑ Ⓒ Ⓓ	41. Ⓐ Ⓑ Ⓒ Ⓓ
8. Ⓐ Ⓑ Ⓒ Ⓓ	25. Ⓐ Ⓑ Ⓒ Ⓓ	42. Ⓐ Ⓑ Ⓒ Ⓓ
9. Ⓐ Ⓑ Ⓒ Ⓓ	26. Ⓐ Ⓑ Ⓒ Ⓓ	43. Ⓐ Ⓑ Ⓒ Ⓓ
10. Ⓐ Ⓑ Ⓒ Ⓓ	27. Ⓐ Ⓑ Ⓒ Ⓓ	44. Ⓐ Ⓑ Ⓒ Ⓓ
11. Ⓐ Ⓑ Ⓒ Ⓓ	28. Ⓐ Ⓑ Ⓒ Ⓓ	45. Ⓐ Ⓑ Ⓒ Ⓓ
12. Ⓐ Ⓑ Ⓒ Ⓓ	29. Ⓐ Ⓑ Ⓒ Ⓓ	46. Ⓐ Ⓑ Ⓒ Ⓓ
13. Ⓐ Ⓑ Ⓒ Ⓓ	30. Ⓐ Ⓑ Ⓒ Ⓓ	47. Ⓐ Ⓑ Ⓒ Ⓓ
14. Ⓐ Ⓑ Ⓒ Ⓓ	31. Ⓐ Ⓑ Ⓒ Ⓓ	48. Ⓐ Ⓑ Ⓒ Ⓓ
15. Ⓐ Ⓑ Ⓒ Ⓓ	32. Ⓐ Ⓑ Ⓒ Ⓓ	49. Ⓐ Ⓑ Ⓒ Ⓓ
16. Ⓐ Ⓑ Ⓒ Ⓓ	33. Ⓐ Ⓑ Ⓒ Ⓓ	50. Ⓐ Ⓑ Ⓒ Ⓓ
17. Ⓐ Ⓑ Ⓒ Ⓓ	34. Ⓐ Ⓑ Ⓒ Ⓓ	51. Ⓐ Ⓑ Ⓒ Ⓓ

52. Ⓐ Ⓑ Ⓒ Ⓓ	55. Ⓐ Ⓑ Ⓒ Ⓓ	58. Ⓐ Ⓑ Ⓒ Ⓓ
53. Ⓐ Ⓑ Ⓒ Ⓓ	56. Ⓐ Ⓑ Ⓒ Ⓓ	59. Ⓐ Ⓑ Ⓒ Ⓓ
54. Ⓐ Ⓑ Ⓒ Ⓓ	57. Ⓐ Ⓑ Ⓒ Ⓓ	60. Ⓐ Ⓑ Ⓒ Ⓓ

ASTRONOMY POST-TEST

Directions: Carefully read each of the following 60 questions. Choose the best answer to each question and fill in the corresponding circle on the answer sheet. The Answer Key and Explanations can be found following this post-test.

1. When we say that a scientific theory needs to be "falsifiable," we mean that scientific theories

   A. will eventually be proved false.
   B. have to include predictions that can be tested.
   C. are not accepted until all their predictions can be tested.
   D. need to be reproducible.

2. Which of the following is NOT part of a good scientific theory?

   A. It cannot be accepted until it has been proven true beyond all doubt.
   B. It must make testable predictions.
   C. It must explain a wide variety of phenomena observed in the natural world.
   D. It should be objective, based on data and evidence, and not based on opinion.

3. Who developed an effective model to predict the positions of planets that remained in use for over 1,500 years?

   A. Galileo Galilei
   B. Tycho Brahe
   C. Ptolemy
   D. Copernicus

4. Kepler's first law of motion states that the planets move in elliptical orbits with the sun at one focus. What is at the other focus of the ellipse?

   A. The earth
   B. Nothing, it is empty
   C. The equant
   D. The satellites/moons of planets

5. If a planet has an orbital period of eight years, according to Kepler's third law, its orbit will have a semi-major axis of

A. 4 AU.
B. 8 AU.
C. 64 AU.
D. 16 AU.

6. According to Kepler's third law, how does a planet's mass affect its orbit around the sun?

A. The more massive the planet, the shorter its orbital period.
B. The more massive the planet, the larger the semi-major axis of its orbit.
C. The more massive the planet, the larger its orbital period.
D. The mass of the planet has no effect on its orbit.

7. How would the gravitational pull of the sun on a planet similar to earth at 10 AU compare to that on earth at 1 AU?

A. 10 times stronger
B. 10 times weaker
C. 100 times stronger
D. 100 times weaker

8. If the sun had 8 times its present mass, what would happen to the gravitational force between the earth and the sun?

A. 8 times stronger
B. 64 times stronger
C. 8 times weaker
D. 16 times stronger

9. If a constant net force is applied to an object, the object will have

A. constant velocity.
B. constant acceleration.
C. increasing speed.
D. increasing acceleration.

10. If you inflate a balloon and then release it while the gas comes out, the balloon will go up. This is an illustration of

A. Newton's first law.
B. Newton's second law.
C. Newton's third law.
D. Newton's law of gravitation.

11. According to Einstein's theory of general relativity, gravity

A. is a force between masses.
B. is the warping of space-time around mass.
C. cannot affect massless particles.
D. is the strongest force.

12. Time in an object traveling at the speed of light will

A. appear to move infinitely slow.
B. appear to move infinitely fast.
C. appear to stop.
D. not be affected by the traveling speed.

13. What are the zodiac constellations?

A. The constellations near the celestial equator
B. The constellations that cross the ecliptic
C. The closest constellations to the solar system
D. The constellations the sun crosses in a month

14. Polaris was not the North Star when the pyramids were built because

A. the eccentricity of the earth's orbit has changed over time.
B. the tilt of the earth's axis has changed over time.
C. the earth's axis points to different parts of the sky over time.
D. Polaris is a young star and was not visible when the pyramids were built.

15. The main component of the atmosphere of earth is

A. oxygen.
B. methane.
C. nitrogen.
D. carbon dioxide.

16. What is true about the moon's orbital and rotational periods?

A. The rotational period is longer than the orbital period.
B. The orbital period is longer than the rotational period.
C. They are equal to the synodic period.
D. The rotational period is equal to the orbital period.

17. When is the earth closest to the sun?

A. June
B. January
C. March
D. September

18. Our month is based on

A. the synodic period of the moon.
B. the rotational period of the moon.
C. the orbital period of the moon.
D. the sidereal period of the moon.

19. Which of the following phenomena of light doesn't agree with the explanation that light is a wave?

A. Reflection
B. Diffraction
C. Refraction
D. Photoelectric effect

20. Which of the following parts of the electromagnetic spectrum has the highest energy?

A. Ultraviolet
B. Visible
C. Gamma
D. X-ray

21. If you double the diameter of a telescope, you will

A. double the resolution and the light-gathering power.
B. increase the resolution and the light-gathering power by four.
C. increase the resolution by four and double the light-gathering power.
D. double the resolution and increase the light-gathering power by four.

22. Light is brought into focus in a refracting telescope by using a

A. concave lens.
B. concave mirror.
C. convex lens.
D. convex mirror.

23. If you observe a distant star, the presence of a cloud of gas between you and the star will produce a(n)

A. absorption spectrum.
B. emission spectrum.
C. continuum spectrum.
D. redshifted spectrum.

24. If you want to know the chemical composition of a star, which piece of information is most useful to you?

A. The peak of emission of its blackbody emission
B. The wavelengths of spectral lines in the star's spectrum
C. The surface color of the star
D. The Doppler shift of the star's spectrum

25. If you look at the spectrum of a star and you see the spectral lines shifted toward the blue, what can you conclude about the star?

A. It is getting hotter.
B. It is getting colder.
C. It is moving toward you.
D. It is moving away from you.

26. If the temperature of a blackbody increases by a factor of 4, the wavelength of the peak of its emission will

A. increase by a factor of 4.
B. increase by a factor of 16.
C. decrease by a factor of 4.
D. decrease by a factor of 16.

27. If the temperature of a blackbody increases by a factor of 3, its energy output will increase by a factor of

A. 81.
B. 9.
C. 6.
D. 3.

28. Venus is so much hotter than earth because it

A. has a much greater amount of carbon dioxide in its atmosphere.
B. is closer to the sun.
C. was formed before the earth.
D. is more massive.

29. Which of the following is farthest from the sun?

A. Pluto
B. Kuiper Belt
C. Oort cloud
D. Asteroid belt

30. Io's surface appears very smooth because it

A. is covered with ice.
B. is liquid.
C. is continually resurfaced by volcanic activity.
D. has been eroded by wind.

31. All Jovian planets

A. are denser than terrestrial planets.
B. have rings around their equators.
C. have only large moons.
D. have weak magnetic fields.

32. Which planet has a rotation period and axis tilt most similar to Earth?

A. Venus
B. Mercury
C. Mars
D. Uranus

33. According to our theory of solar system formation, why do all the planets orbit the sun in the same direction and in nearly the same plane?

A. The laws of conservation of energy and angular momentum ensure that any rotating, collapsing cloud will end up as a spinning disk.
B. Any planets that once orbited in the opposite direction or in a different plane were ejected from the solar system.
C. The sun formed first, and as it grew in size it spread into a disk, rather like the way a ball of dough can be flattened into a pizza by spinning it.
D. This is one of many possible configurations, and we would expect planets in other solar systems to have a different pattern.

34. In essence, the nebular theory states that

A. nebulae are clouds of gas and dust in space.
B. our solar system formed from the collapse of an interstellar cloud of gas and dust.
C. the planets each formed from the collapse of its own separate nebula.
D. all low-mass stars will end their lives as planetary nebulae.

35. The gravitational microlensing method for detecting an extrasolar planet relies on

A. a planet passing in front of its host star and blocking a small portion of the star's light.
B. the velocity of the host star changing due to the gravitational pull from the planet.
C. the slight deflection of light and apparent brightening of a star that can occur when a star aligns with another star that has its own planet in our line of sight.
D. the position of a star changing slightly due to the gravitational pull from the planet.

36. The spectrum of planets can be roughly divided into two components: one part that peaks in the optical due to

A. reflection of starlight, and one part that peaks in the infrared due to thermal radiation from the planet.
B. thermal radiation from the planet, and one part that peaks in the infrared due to reflection of star light.
C. reflection of starlight, and one part that peaks in the radio due to thermal radiation from the planet.
D. reflection of starlight, and one part that peaks in the infrared due to reflection of infrared radiation from the star.

37. What primarily determines the location of a habitable zone around a star?

A. The age of the star
B. The luminosity of the star
C. The mass of the star
D. The spectral type of the star

38. What is the definition of a star's habitable zone?

A. The range of distances from a star where liquid water can be stable on the surface of a suitable planet
B. The range of distances from a star where terrestrial planets can form
C. The range of distances from a star where organic molecules can be stable on the surface of a suitable planet
D. The regions in a planetary system where there is liquid water

39. How will the habitable zone of a star more luminous than the sun compare to the habitable zone in our solar system?

A. Same
B. Wider and closer to the star
C. Narrower and farther away from the star
D. Wider and farther away from the star

40. What are the layers of the solar atmosphere?

A. Convection zone, radiation zone, and corona
B. Radiation zone, photosphere, and chromosphere
C. Photosphere, chromosphere, and corona
D. Chromosphere, corona, and solar wind

41. If the sunspot cycle reaches a minimum in 2019, when will we expect to see a large number of sunspots on its surface?

A. 2030
B. 2041
C. 2025
D. It is impossible to know.

42. Three M-class stars are identified as being main sequence, giant, and supergiant stars, respectively. In what physical property do they differ?

A. Luminosity
B. Spectral class
C. Color
D. Surface temperature

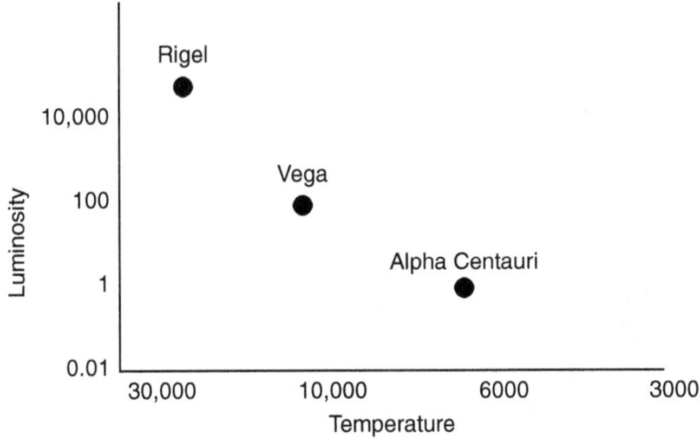

43. The HR diagram image provided above has temperature in Kelvin on the horizontal axis and luminosity in solar luminosities on the vertical axis. All the stars in the diagram are in the main sequence. Which of the stars will have a lifetime longer than the lifetime of our sun?

A. Rigel
B. Rigel and Vega
C. Rigel, Vega, and Alpha Centauri
D. None

44. Two stars have the same temperature with one having twice the radius of the other. The larger star is

A. four times as luminous.
B. four times less luminous.
C. twice as luminous.
D. half as luminous.

45. A planetary nebula results when

A. a planet loses its atmosphere due to weak gravity.
B. a cloud of gas and dust collapses to make a planet.
C. a low-mass star ejects its outer layers at the end of fusion.
D. a red giant swallows the inner planets as it expands.

46. Suppose a white dwarf in a binary system is accreting mass from its companion. What happens to the white dwarf if its mass reaches the 1.4 solar mass limit?

A. It becomes a nova.
B. It collapses into a black hole.
C. It detonates as a supernova.
D. It starts fusion again.

47. A star 100 times the mass of the sun will end its life as a

A. neutron star.
B. black hole.
C. white dwarf.
D. planetary nebula.

48. Where is the carbon in the universe produced?

A. Only inside massive stars
B. Only in supernova explosions
C. In the big bang
D. Inside all stars

49. What type of galaxy is the Milky Way?

A. Spherical
B. Elliptical
C. Spiral
D. Barred spiral

50. Globular clusters in our galaxy are

A. found mostly in the disk of the galaxy.
B. found mostly in the bulge of the galaxy.
C. made only of old stars.
D. made of stars of high metallicity.

51. Which is true about elliptical and spiral galaxies?

A. Spiral galaxies have a spherical component, a disk with spiral arms, and active star formation, while elliptical galaxies have a spherical component and no active star formation.
B. Spiral galaxies only have a disk with spiral arms and active star formation, while elliptical galaxies only have a spherical component and no active star formation.
C. Spiral galaxies have a spherical component with spiral arms and no active star formation, while elliptical galaxies have a spherical component and active star formation.
D. Spiral galaxies have a spiral disk and no active star formation, while elliptical galaxies have a spherical component and no active star formation.

52. Which type of galaxy contains the least amount of interstellar material and star formation?

A. Spirals
B. Barred spirals
C. Irregulars
D. Ellipticals

53. What is the distance to a star with a parallax angle of 0.025 arcseconds?

A. 4 light years
B. 40 light years
C. 25 parsecs
D. 40 parsecs

54. What is the distance to a galaxy with a radial velocity of 720 km/s if the Hubble constant is 72 km/s per Mpc?

A. 100 Mpc
B. 10 Mpc
C. 10 light years
D. 100 light years

55. Which is true about galaxy clusters?

A. Most of the cluster mass is in the form of a superhot gas in the center.
B. They are the largest structures in the universe bound by gravity.
C. They all have a very large galaxy in the center of the cluster with smaller galaxies in larger orbits.
D. They all have hundreds of galaxies.

56. What is an important cosmological implication of Hubble's law?

A. The universe is infinite.
B. The universe had a beginning.
C. The universe will expand forever.
D. The expansion of the universe is accelerating.

57. The afterglow of the very hot universe after the big bang can be seen today as radiation in the

A. microwave part of the spectrum.
B. X-ray part of the spectrum.
C. visible part of the spectrum.
D. infrared part of the spectrum.

58. If the expansion of the universe accelerates forever, what would we be able to tell about its density?

A. Much higher than the critical density
B. Equal to the critical density
C. Close to the critical density
D. Much lower than the critical density

59. Based on current evidence, what fraction of the universe is dark energy?

A. 50%
B. 25%
C. 70%
D. 5%

60. Most of the mass of the universe is contained in

A. large clouds of gas.
B. very massive O and B stars.
C. very low-mass stars.
D. invisible dark matter.

ANSWER KEY AND EXPLANATIONS

1. B	13. B	25. C	37. B	49. D
2. A	14. C	26. C	38. A	50. C
3. C	15. C	27. A	39. D	51. A
4. B	16. D	28. A	40. C	52. D
5. A	17. B	29. C	41. C	53. D
6. D	18. A	30. C	42. A	54. B
7. D	19. D	31. B	43. D	55. B
8. A	20. C	32. C	44. A	56. B
9. B	21. D	33. A	45. C	57. A
10. C	22. C	34. B	46. C	58. D
11. B	23. A	35. C	47. B	59. C
12. C	24. B	36. A	48. D	60. D

1. **The correct answer is B.** Scientific theories must include testable predictions, making them "falsifiable." Choice A is incorrect because not all scientific theories will prove to be false at some point. Choice C is incorrect because a theory could be accepted before all its predictions can be tested. Choice D is incorrect; "falsifiable" and "reproducible" are not synonyms.

2. **The correct answer is A.** A scientific theory will never be proven beyond all doubt. New discoveries and observations will provide new methods to test theories. All scientific theories need to be falsifiable (choice B), explain a variety of natural phenomena (choice C), and be objective (choice D).

3. **The correct answer is C.** Ptolemy developed a geocentric model of the universe that accurately predicted the position of planets and remained the standard model for over 1,500 years. Galileo (choice A) did not create his own model of the universe; he supported the heliocentric model proposed by Copernicus. The model of the universe proposed by Tycho Brahe (choice B) was only popular for a short period of time. While Copernicus (choice D) created a heliocentric model of the solar system, the model represented the motion of the planets with circles, and it was quickly modified once Kepler showed that the planetary orbits were elliptical.

4. **The correct answer is B.** Kepler's first law says that the planets move in elliptical orbits with the sun occupying one of the two foci, while the other focus remains empty. Neither the earth (choice A) nor satellites (choice D) are on one focus. The equant (choice C) was used by Ptolemy to explain the variable rate of motion of planets and is not used by Kepler.

5. **The correct answer is A.** According to Kepler's third law of planetary motion, the square of the orbital period of a planet is equal to the cube of its semi-major axis. If the planet has a period of 8 years, its orbit will have a semi-major axis of 4 AU because $8^2 = 4^3$. All other choices are incorrect.

6. **The correct answer is D.** Kepler's third law of planetary motion states that the square of the orbital period of a planet is equal to the cube of its semi-major axis, and it doesn't include the mass of the planet. His law can be accurately used for planets orbiting the sun because the masses of the planets are negligible compared to the mass of the sun. Choices A, B, and C are incorrect because Kepler's third law doesn't include planetary mass.

7. **The correct answer is D.** The force of gravity depends on the inverse of the square of the distance. Therefore, if the distance is 10 times larger, the gravitational force will be 100 times weaker. All other choices are incorrect.

8. **The correct answer is A.** The force of gravity is directly proportional to the mass of the objects. Therefore, if the mass is eight times larger, the gravitational force will be eight times stronger. All other choices are incorrect.

9. **The correct answer is B.** According to Newton's second law, the law of force, force equals mass times acceleration. If a constant net force is applied to an object, the object will have a constant acceleration. Choice A is incorrect because a constant force will produce a change in the velocity of the object. Choice C is incorrect because, while a constant force will result in a change in velocity, that change could be an increase or decrease in speed or a change in the direction of motion. Choice D is incorrect because an increasing acceleration will require an increasing force.

10. **The correct answer is C.** Newton's third law, the law of reaction, states that for every action there is an equal but opposite reaction. In this instance, the balloon pushes the gas downward as it leaves the balloon, and that gas pushes the balloon upward. Newton's first law (choice A) is the law of inertia, and his second law (choice B) is the law of force, neither of which are illustrated by the example. The law of gravitation (choice D) doesn't play a role in the scenario presented above.

11. **The correct answer is B.** According to Einstein's theory of general relativity, masses distort the space-time around them, and gravity is what we experience as a result of the warping of space-time. This explains why light can be affected by gravity even when photons, the particles of light, have no mass. Choice A is incorrect because in general relativity, even if a mass is zero, it can be affected by gravity. Gravity can affect massless particles, so choice C is incorrect. Choice D is incorrect because gravity is a relatively weak force compared to the other three fundamental forces.

12. **The correct answer is C.** According to Einstein's theory of special relativity, time and space are relative. Time appears to slow down the faster we travel, and it seems to completely stop when the speed of light is reached. Choices A and B are incorrect because time will appear to completely stop at the speed of light. Choice D is incorrect because time is relative to velocity and is therefore affected by how fast we travel.

13. **The correct answer is B.** As the sun travels in the ecliptic, it crosses 13 constellations. These constellations are known as the zodiac constellations, which form a band centered on the ecliptic. All other choices are incorrect.

14. **The correct answer is C.** The axis of rotation of earth precesses like a spinning top with a period of 26,000 years. Because of this, the North Pole points to different regions of the sky, completing a large circle in 26,000 years. During the time the Egyptian pyramids were built, the axis of earth was pointing towards the star Thuban. Choice A is incorrect because the eccentricity of the earth's orbit doesn't change where the North Pole points. Choice B is incorrect because the axis tilt of earth changes very little over a period of 40,000 years, and the effect is not significant compared to the precession of the earth's axis. Choice D is incorrect because Polaris was also visible during the time of the pyramids.

15. **The correct answer is C.** The atmosphere of earth is 78% nitrogen, 21% oxygen, ~1% water vapor and carbon. Oxygen (choice A) is only 21% of the earth's atmosphere. Methane (choice B) and carbon dioxide (choice D) are trace gases and account for less than 0.1% of the earth's atmosphere.

16. **The correct answer is D.** The moon completes one rotation on its axis at the same time that it completes one orbit around earth. The moon's rotational and orbital period are also equal to the sidereal period of the moon, which is 27.3 days. Choices A and B are incorrect because the rotational and orbital period are the same. The synodic period (choice C) of the moon is 29.5 days, which is longer than the orbital and rotational period.

17. **The correct answer is B.** The earth is closest to the sun in January and farthest from the sun in July. All other choices are incorrect.

18. **The correct answer is A.** The month in our calendar is based on the period of the lunar phases, which is called the synodic period of the moon. The synodic period of the moon is 29.5 days. The rotational (choice B), orbital (choice C), and sidereal periods (choice D) of the moon are identical (27.3 days), and our month is based on the lunar phases.

19. **The correct answer is D.** When light is projected onto a metal plate, electrons can absorb the photons and be ejected, creating electricity. This is called the photoelectric effect. Since only photons of specific energies are absorbed, this effect cannot be explained by using waves. All waves can be reflected (choice A), refracted (choice C), and diffracted (choice B).

20. **The correct answer is C.** The different parts of the electromagnetic spectrum in order of decreasing energy are gamma rays, X-rays, ultraviolet, visible, infrared, microwave, and radio. Therefore, gamma rays have the highest energy, highest frequency, and shortest wavelength. Ultraviolet (choice A), visible (choice B), and X-rays (choice D) have lower energy than gamma.

21. **The correct answer is D.** The resolution of a telescope is directly proportional to the diameter, while the light-gathering power is proportional to the light-collecting area, which depends on the diameter squared. If the diameter of a telescope doubles, the resolution will also double, but the light-gathering power will increase by $2^2 = 4$. All other choices are incorrect.

22. **The correct answer is C.** A refracting telescope uses convex lenses, which cause light rays to converge and come into focus, creating an image. A concave lens (choice A) makes the light rays diverge and will not create an image. Choices B and D are incorrect because a refracting telescope uses lenses instead of mirrors.

23. **The correct answer is A.** A low-density medium (a cloud of gas) between the observer and a hot, dense source (star) will create an absorption spectrum. For us to see an emission spectrum (choice B), the cloud needs to be hotter than the background, and in this scenario we have a star behind the cloud. A cloud of gas has low density, and it won't produce a continuum spectrum (choice C). To produce a redshifted spectrum (choice D), an object needs to be moving away from us.

24. **The correct answer is B.** Each element and molecule has spectral lines that are unique to that element or molecule. If we want to identify the chemical composition of a star, we need to observe and measure the position of the spectral lines. The peak of emission of a blackbody (choice A) will tell us the temperature of a star, but not its composition. The surface color of the star (choice C) is also related to the temperature and not the composition. The Doppler shift of a star's spectrum (choice D) will provide information on its motion toward or away from us, but not its composition.

25. **The correct answer is C.** If the lines in the spectrum are shifted toward the blue (shorter) wavelengths, this means that the object is moving toward us. Choices A and B are incorrect because the lines will not shift due to a change in temperature. If the star was moving away from us (choice D), the lines would be shifted toward the red (longer) wavelengths, not toward the blue.

26. **The correct answer is C.** The wavelength of the peak of emission of a blackbody is inversely proportional to the temperature of the object. Therefore, if the temperature increases by a factor of 4, the wavelength of the peak of emission will decrease by a factor of 4. Choices A and B are incorrect because the wavelength will *decrease* by a factor of 4, not increase. Choice D is incorrect because the wavelength will decrease by 4 and not by 16.

27. **The correct answer is A.** The energy output of a blackbody per unit area is proportional to its temperature to the fourth power. If the temperature increases by a factor of 3, its energy output will increase by 3^4, or 81. All the other choices are incorrect.

28. **The correct answer is A.** Venus has a very large amount of carbon dioxide in its atmosphere, producing a greenhouse effect that doesn't let radiation from the planet escape into space. Even though Venus is closer to the sun than earth (choice B), that alone is not enough to explain the difference in temperature. Choice C is incorrect because the planets in our solar system formed mostly at the same time, and choice D is incorrect because the earth is slightly more massive than Venus.

29. **The correct answer is C.** The Oort cloud is a spherical region surrounding the solar system beyond the Kuiper Belt. It is the place of origin of long-period comets. Pluto (choice A) is an object in the Kuiper Belt, and the Oort cloud is beyond the Kuiper Belt (choice B). The asteroid belt (choice D) is between the orbits of Mars and Jupiter, much closer to the sun than the Oort cloud.

30. **The correct answer is C.** Io, one of the Galilean moons, is the most volcanically active body in the solar system. Its surface is constantly renovated by volcanic activity. The surface of Io is not covered with ice (choice A), nor does it consist of liquid (choice B). Erosion by wind (choice D) doesn't play a role in Io.

31. **The correct answer is B.** All Jovian planets have rings around their equators. Choice A is incorrect because all Jovian planets are less dense than terrestrial planets. Choice C is incorrect because all Jovian planets have small and large moons, and choice D is incorrect because all Jovian planets have strong magnetic fields.

32. **The correct answer is C.** Mars has a rotation period of 24.6 hours, less than an hour longer than earth's rotation period, and it has an axis tilt of about 25 degrees, less than two degrees off from the earth's tilt (23.5 degrees). Venus (choice A) has a rotation period of 243 days, the longest day of any planet in the solar system, and an axis tilt of only 3 degrees. Mercury (choice B) has a rotation period of 59 days and an axis tilt of only 2 degrees. Uranus (choice D), as all Jovian planets, rotates very fast (17 hours) and has an axis tilt of almost 98 degrees.

33. **The correct answer is A.** The solar system formed from a large cloud of gas and dust. As the rotating cloud collapsed, conservation of energy and angular momentum shaped the cloud into a spinning disk from which all the planets formed. Choice B is incorrect because all planets formed from the same disk, and therefore we expect most of the planets to be in the same plane and orbit in the same direction, unless altered by some external event. Choice C is incorrect because the sun will not spread into a disk, and planets were forming while the sun was forming. Choice D is incorrect since conservation of energy and angular momentum will have similar outcomes in other solar systems.

34. **The correct answer is B.** The nebular theory explains the formation of the solar system from a collapsing cloud of gas and dust. Even though nebulae are clouds of gas and dust (choice A), and all low-mass stars will go through a planetary nebulae stage at the end of their lives (choice D), that is not what the nebular theory states. Choice C is incorrect because all planets in the solar system formed from the same collapsing cloud.

35. **The correct answer is C.** Microlensing happens because a mass warps the space around itself. If a star plus a star and planet are aligned to our line of sight, we will see an increase in the brightness of the star and planet, allowing us to detect a faint planet close to a star. The other choices are incorrect because they all refer to other methods of detecting planets: choice A refers to the transit method, choice B refers to the Doppler method, and choice D refers to the astrometry method.

36. **The correct answer is A.** The surface of a planet will reflect part of the light it receives from the star. This reflected light will peak in the optical part of the spectrum. Planets also absorb part of the radiation they receive, and as a result they warm up and emit their own thermal radiation which peaks at longer wavelengths (the infrared part of the spectrum). All other choices are incorrect.

37. **The correct answer is B.** The luminosity of a star, or its total output of energy per second, determines the size of the surrounding region where a planet could have stable liquid water on the surface. Stars of different ages (choice A) can have the same luminosity, as can stars of different masses (choice C) or different spectral types (choice D).

38. **The correct answer is A.** The habitable zone is the range of distances around a star where liquid water could be stable on the surface of a planet. Choice B is incorrect because terrestrial planets can form outside the habitable zone. Organic molecules can be stable outside the habitable zone, so choice C is incorrect. Choice D is incorrect because liquid water could be present outside the habitable zone.

39. **The correct answer is D.** The habitable zone of a more luminous star will be wider and farther from the star. Choice A is incorrect because the location and size of the habitable zone changes with the luminosity of the star. Choice B is incorrect because it will have to be farther from the more luminous star to have the correct temperatures for liquid water. Choice C is incorrect because the habitable zone for a more luminous star will be wider, not narrower.

40. **The correct answer is C.** The solar atmosphere is composed of the photosphere, the chromosphere, and the corona. Choice A and choice B are incorrect because the convection zone and the radiation zone are both interior layers of the sun. Choice D is incorrect because the solar wind is not one of the layers of the atmosphere of the sun.

41. **The correct answer is C.** The sunspot cycle lasts 11 years, at which point the polarity of the sunspots reverses, and a new cycle begins. If the sun is at a minimum in 2019, the maximum is expected five and a half years from 2019, in 2025. The year 2030 (choice A) is 11 years after 2019, and 2041 (choice B) is 22 years after 2019; both of these years are on the same part of the 11-year cycle, so a minimum of activity is expected. Choice D is incorrect because the sunspot cycle is regular and reliable, making it easy to predict when we will see a maximum or a minimum.

42. The correct answer is A. The luminosity of a star depends on its temperature as well as its size. If the three stars have the same spectral type, M, but have different sizes, then they will have different luminosities. Choices B, C, and D are incorrect because they all have the same spectral class, M, and therefore they have the same surface temperature and color.

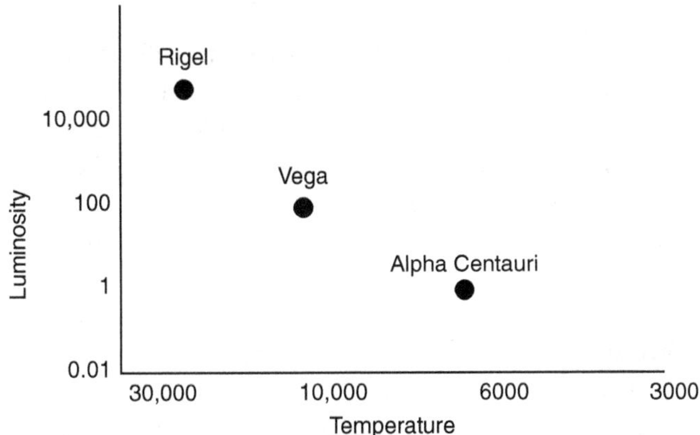

43. The correct answer is D. The sun, like Alpha Centauri, has a temperature of about 6,000 Kelvin. Since all the stars in the diagram are in the main sequence and have temperatures equal to or higher than our sun, they will also have masses equal to or higher than our sun. The lifetime of a star is longer for less massive stars; therefore, none of the stars in the diagram will have longer lifetimes. All the other choices are incorrect.

44. The correct answer is A. The luminosity of a star is proportional to the fourth power of effective temperature and its radius squared. If two stars have the same temperature, but one has a radius twice as large as the other, the surface area and luminosity of the larger star will be four times larger. All other choices are incorrect.

45. The correct answer is C. A planetary nebula is one of the last stages of evolution for a low-mass star. All the other choices are incorrect.

46. **The correct answer is C.** Once the mass of a white dwarf reaches 1.4 solar masses, the white dwarf will explode as a supernova and be destroyed in the process. For a nova (choice A), the mass needs to stay below 1.4 solar masses. A white dwarf (choice B) will never become a black hole. The white dwarf will not be stable, and it will be destroyed when it reaches the 1.4 solar mass limit, unable to start fusion again (choice D).

47. **The correct answer is B.** The most massive stars will detonate as Type II supernovae at the end of their lives, and if their core mass is above four solar masses, they will become black holes. For a star to become a neutron star (choice A), its core mass needs to be between 1.4 and four solar masses. Planetary nebula (choice D) and white dwarf (choice C) are stages of the evolution of low-mass stars.

48. **The correct answer is D.** Carbon is produced inside all stars by nuclear fusion. Choice A is incorrect because carbon is also produced in low-mass stars like our sun. Choice B is incorrect because carbon is fused inside all stars. Choice C is incorrect because while hydrogen and helium were produced mostly in the first few minutes after the big bang, carbon is made inside stars.

49. **The correct answer is D.** The Milky Way is a barred spiral galaxy. It has a halo with globular clusters, a disk, a bar close to the center from which spiral arms come out, and a bulge around the central region. We do not classify galaxies as spherical (choice A). Elliptical galaxies (choice B) do not have disks or spiral arms. The Milky Way has a bar through the center, making it a barred spiral galaxy rather than just a spiral galaxy (choice C).

50. **The correct answer is C.** Stars that make the globular clusters are old. Globular clusters are found in the halo of the galaxy, not in the disk (choice A) or the central bulge (choice B). Choice D is incorrect because stars in the globular clusters have low metallicities.

51. **The correct answer is A.** Spiral galaxies have a spherical component or halo with globular clusters made of old stars. They have a disk with spiral arms where star formation takes place. Elliptical galaxies only have the spherical component and no star formation. All the other choices are incorrect.

52. The correct answer is D. Ellipticals have the least amount of interstellar material and no star formation. Spirals (choice A), barred spirals (choice B), and irregulars (choice C) have large amounts of interstellar material and active star formation.

53. The correct answer is D. The distance to a star in units of parsecs is equal to the inverse of its parallax angle in units of arcseconds. Therefore, a star with a parallax angle of 0.025 arcseconds will be 40 parsecs away. Choice B is incorrect because a light year is different from a parsec. Choices A and C give the wrong distance.

54. The correct answer is B. Distances to galaxies can be found by dividing the radial velocity of the galaxy by the Hubble constant. A galaxy moving at 720 km/s will have a distance of 10 Mpc because 720 km/s divided by 72 km/s per Mpc is equal to 10 Mpc. All the other choices are incorrect.

55. The correct answer is B. Galaxy clusters are the largest structures still bound by gravity. Choice A is incorrect because most of the mass in a galaxy cluster is dark matter. Choice C is incorrect because the centers of galaxy clusters are occupied by superhot gas. Choice D is incorrect because galaxy clusters can be small. Our own galaxy cluster has close to 40 galaxies.

56. The correct answer is B. Hubble's law states that the farther a galaxy is from us, the faster it is moving away. This expansion of the universe implies that the universe was smaller in the past and had a definite beginning. The universe doesn't have to be infinite (choice A) according to Hubble's law. We don't know if the universe will expand forever (choice C). Hubble's law only tells us about the expansion of the universe, not if the rate of expansion is changing with time (choice D).

57. The correct answer is A. Because of the expansion of the universe, the afterglow of the very hot early universe is seen today at much longer wavelengths in the microwave part of the electromagnetic spectrum, and it is called cosmic microwave background (CMB) radiation. Choices B, C, and D are incorrect because the radiation is in the microwave area of spectrum, not in the X-ray, visible, or infrared spectrums.

58. **The correct answer is D.** If the expansion of the universe accelerates forever, we know that the universe doesn't have enough density to slow down the expansion, stop the expansion, or reverse it. The density needed to stop the expansion is called the critical density. If the density was much higher than the critical density (choice A), the expansion would stop, and the universe would collapse back onto itself. If the density of the universe was equal to the critical density (choice B), the expansion of the universe would stop, and the universe would reach a stable size. If the density of the universe was close to the critical density (choice C), the expansion of the universe would slow down over time.

59. **The correct answer is C.** Based on our current estimates, the universe is 68% dark energy, 27% dark matter, and only about 5% normal matter. All the other choices are incorrect.

60. **The correct answer is D.** Most of the mass of the universe is in the form of dark matter. This dark matter makes up 25% of the total content of the universe, while luminous matter makes up only 5% of the total content of the universe. Choices A, B, and C are incorrect because they are all forms of luminous matter.

Printed in the USA
CPSIA information can be obtained
at www.ICGtesting.com
JSHW012041140824
68134JS00033B/3191